Reality TV star and influencer Georgia Harrison has appeared on *Love Island*, *The Only Way is Essex*, *Ex on the Beach* and *The Challenge*. Since her very public trial against her ex-boyfriend she has gained thousands of new fans and supporters around the world, who applaud and support her bravery in what has been regarded as a huge win for women. In navigating what was a deeply challenging period of her life, Georgia has come out stronger, and more resilient than ever, with a real desire to help others. As an ardent campaigner for causes relating to online safety regulations and privacy, Georgia has fought relentlessly to have her message, and those of the people she's standing with, heard to great effect.

TAKING BACK MY POWER

Georgia Harrison

ЯENE
GADE

RENEGADE BOOKS

First published in Great Britain in 2023 by Renegade Books

1 3 5 7 9 10 8 6 4 2

A CIP catalogue record for this book
is available from the British Library.

ISBN 978-0-349-13100-9

Typeset in Berling by M Rules
Printed and bound in Great Britain by
Clays Ltd, Elcograf S.p.A

Papers used by Renegade Books are from well-managed forests
and other responsible sources.

MIX
Supporting
responsible forestry
FSC® C104740
FSC
www.fsc.org

Renegade Books
An imprint of Dialogue
Carmelite House
50 Victoria Embankment
London EC4Y 0DZ

An Hachette UK Company
www.hachette.co.uk

www.dialoguebooks.co.uk

Renegade Books, part of Little, Brown, Book Group Limited,
an Hachette UK company.

This book is dedicated to my mum,
my absolute rock in life. Thank you for
being with me every step of the way.
I love you.

CONTENTS

'THIS IS NOT A
SAD STORY.

IT'S A STORY ABOUT
THE POWER OF HOPE.'

'EVERY THOUGHT HAS A POWER. IF YOU'RE GOING TO AIM, AIM BIG – AND WHEN YOU GET THERE, ENJOY THE MOMENT. OWN IT. YOU'VE CREATED IT. YOU DESERVE IT.'

Prologue

TAKING BACK
MY HOPES

MUM'S GARDEN, ESSEX, 11 P.M., JULY 2022

I don't want to be here. I don't see the point in being on this earth anymore. I want to be up there in the sky. With the stars. With my best boy-mate, Cenk, and my ex-boyfriend Jake.

But I'm here. I'm slumped on my back in the grass. My body's present but my soul is switched off. I see myself from above: a girl of twenty-seven, lost in a baggy track-suit I've lived in for days. My unwashed hair is a matted ball on the top of my head, and my eyes have swollen like golf balls from crying so much. My face shines wet in the moonlight. A wine glass lies limply in my hand, Sauvignon Blanc sloshing onto the lawn. I see all my hopes draining away to nothing.

I don't want to be here.

I hear noises. Crying, screaming, pleading. Warm hands land on my forehead, then my shoulders.

'Georgia, please, come inside. You can't stay here all night. Please, Georgia, sweetie. I need you to get up ... for yourself, for me, for us.'

Mum's voice sounds like it's coming from afar, from a deep tunnel somewhere inside the house behind me. I can't move. I can't speak. I can't think. *I don't care about anything right now.*

This has been my state of mind since my friend Tyla called me – *was it two, three or even four days ago?* – with news that ripped my world apart.

'Oh, God, Georgia, have you heard what happened?' she'd said. 'Jake drove off a cliff in Turkey yesterday. He broke his neck and died instantly.'

'What, d'you mean Jake McLean?' I could barely get the words out. In my mind I knew Tyla was telling me that Jake McLean, who'd been my on-off boyfriend for the last ten years, was dead. But I didn't want to believe it. *No, not my Jake! The funniest, cheekiest man you could ever meet. Everybody loves Jake – he has the most magical personality. Please, no ...* My whole body went into shock. Shaking uncontrollably, I dropped my phone, threw myself onto my bed and screamed hysterically into the pillow for hours. I've been inconsolable ever since.

I can't get through this, I really can't. My grief is unsurmountable. Jake's passing has come nearly seven months after my best friend, Cenk Fahri, died after fighting a ten-year battle against cancer. Cenk was the same age as me and we'd been inseparable since the moment we'd met back in 2006, on my first day at Roding Valley High School, when he'd flashed me his mischievous grin and said, 'I'm going to look after you, Gee.' We spent literally every day together. He was just the most decent human being: kind, funny, selfless and true to his word. Cenk looked after me, always – right down to his final days in hospital.

Cenk and Jake were the two men who were there for me, the people I could trust and rely on. Tonight, as Mum continues to beg me to get up, I wonder, *Will I ever heal?* I was just regaining some semblance of normality after losing Cenk, and now . . . this.

'Georgia, please, I'm begging you.' Mum's shaking me now. Still, I don't move. I have no idea how long I've been here, sprawled on the grass. I have fuzzy recollections of the evening, of sitting around the garden table with Mum and my girlfriends, drinking glass after glass of wine but not feeling anywhere near drunk enough to dampen my pain. Repeatedly playing Ed Sheeran's 'Perfect' on my phone, wailing at the lyrics that once belonged to Jake and me. 'Perfect' was *our* song.

When did my friends leave? When did the moon and stars replace the sun? I haven't a clue, but the two brightest stars in the clear night sky are all I can see. They're all that I want to see – because I decide that one star is Cenk and the other, Jake.

'I want to stay here, with Cenk and Jake,' I tell Mum. My voice is unrecognisably deep and jagged; my breath smells of sour wine. 'I can't leave them. I want to be with Cenk and Jake. I want to be with Cenk and Jake. I *have* to be with . . .'

I feel as though I'm flooding the garden with my tears. The stars are zigzagging in a pool of navy ink, and suddenly I'm rising, surrendering to Mum's grasp around my waist as she half carries me indoors. 'That's it, sweetie, we've got this,' she says.

Next thing, Mum's tucking me into her bed, but I don't remember climbing the stairs. There's literally nothing left in me. Mum kisses my forehead then opens the balcony doors opposite the bed.

'There you go,' she says. 'Now you can see the stars again. You can be with Cenk and Jake.'

Mum gets into bed with me, kisses my head again. 'We'll get through this, Georgia, I promise. Things won't stay this way forever.'

Silent tears soak my face. The two stars flicker in and out of focus as I close my eyes. *I don't want to be here.*

When I look back on those days following Jake's death, I ask myself, *How did a young girl, full of hope and love and positivity, find herself in such a desperate situation?* It scares me to think of the dark depths of grief I'd plunged into. Honestly, lying there in my mum, Nicola's garden that night, I couldn't imagine ever smiling again, let alone facing another day. There wasn't anything anybody could have said to lift me. My brain wasn't functioning properly – that's what intense grief does to you. I know as much now, but I had no idea at the time. Back then, I didn't want to be there. I wanted to fade away, disappear.

Those were rock-bottom times, without a shadow of a doubt. But I was also dealing with another trauma – one inflicted upon me by Stephen Bear, fellow reality-TV star, winner of series 17 of *Celebrity Big Brother* in 2016 and my narcissistic ex-boyfriend.

In August 2020, after a drunken reunion at Bear's house in Loughton, Essex, he secretly filmed himself having sex with me in his garden. Then, without my consent, Bear uploaded the CCTV footage to his *OnlyFans* site, adding a caption along the lines of: *Sign up now for 50 per cent off to see me fucking this bitch in my garden.* I felt violated, exploited. By sharing this intimate footage of me, Bear took away my innocence and dignity. He ruined my life for no other reason than financial gain and presumably to boost his already-inflated ego. How could he do this to me?

So, as I struggled to process the shock of Jake's death, so soon after Cenk's passing, I also faced confronting Bear in a packed courtroom. After I reported the matter to police – and waived my anonymity – Bear was charged with two counts of disclosing private sex photos or film and one count of voyeurism. Of course, he'd pleaded not guilty to all charges and his (postponed) trial was due to start in December 2022.

Amid my all-consuming grief, I was terrified at the prospect of coming face to face with Bear in court. My faith was shattered. *What if he swans into the courtroom, tells a pack of lies and gets exonerated? How can I rebuild my faith in humanity and the universe in the short amount of time I have to get my shit together?*

A few days after my garden episode, I spoke to Mum about Bear's forthcoming trial.

'I can't do it, Mum. I can't go to court. I can't be strong anymore. I'm a broken woman,' I said. 'I can't face what's coming. Having to go up against Bear, up against the cameras, the press . . . I just don't know where I'm going to find the strength for that.'

Mum, bless her, wrapped me in her arms. 'Look, we're not looking for strength for that right now, sweetie. We're just looking for the strength to get up in the morning. To get into the shower, get dressed, eat breakfast. This is what we're finding the strength to do, and we'll take one day at a time.'

I cried into Mum's shoulder, her words igniting in me the first glimmer of hope I'd felt in days. 'I hope so,' I sniffed, and picked up my phone. I'd been glued to it twenty-four-seven, listening to 'Perfect' on *YouTube*, scrolling obsessively through my last text messages from Jake. Sobbing while swiping through hundreds of photographs of me with Jake and Cenk. 'I really hope so.'

How I got through that awful time in my life, I'll never know, but somehow, I did – thanks to my amazing mum and friends who would guide me along the perilous path ahead. I relinquished my phone to my agent, Neil, and slowly began to regain my hopes. My addiction to self-help books was also pivotal in restoring my faith. 'Trust the universe,' I began to tell myself. 'You've got this.'

A week later, I flew out to Los Angeles with my little stepsister, Darcey, who was then seventeen. My friend Ahmad had invited us to stay with him for six weeks. I was looking forward to getting away from it all – a change of scene was just what I needed to kick-start the healing process.

Soon after take-off, I opened my notebook and began writing. Once I started, I couldn't stop. I spilled all my emotions on to the page. Darcey nudged me when I was mid-flow. 'Oi, Georgia, what are you doing?' she asked. 'C'mon, let's play cards.'

I cast her a sideways smile – my first smile in a long while. 'I'm writing a book.'

Darcey laughed into her copy of *Heat* magazine. 'Oh, fuck off, you're so *not* writing a book.'

'I am,' I replied.

Truth was, I didn't know where my path was leading. In hindsight, I realise I had an underlying faith burning inside of me. I knew that, despite my agony and grief, I could pull through this, take back my hopes and manifest into a better version of myself. *If I'm strong enough, everything will align one day*, I thought, and continued writing at a frenzied pace.

I can't believe that my dream of writing a book has come true – and you're reading it now.

This is not a sad story. It's a story about the power of hope, and how I managed, with resilience and faith, to navigate myself through my lowest times.

This is my journey.

'THE UNIVERSE IS
MIRRORING YOUR
INNER THOUGHTS
AND FEELINGS BACK
TO YOU. CHANGE THE
WAY YOU LOOK AT
YOURSELF, AND THE
WORLD WILL CHANGE
HOW IT LOOKS.'

'TO MANIFEST WHAT YOU WANT, YOU HAVE TO DECIDE FOR YOURSELF WHAT THIS IS. THE PROBLEM IS, MOST PEOPLE ARE TOO SCARED TO DREAM BIG, OR TO IMAGINE A LIFE BETTER THAN THEIR CURRENT REALITY. DON'T BE MOST PEOPLE.'

Chapter One

TAKING BACK
MY DREAMS

CALA BASSA BEACH CLUB,
IBIZA, SEPTEMBER 2014

'Okay, George, you know what you're doing, right? You'll take a short walk along the beach until you reach the two girls on the sunbeds over there ... then do your thing, just be yourself.'

The geezer wearing giant bug-like headphones swung his clipboard diagonally right. Squinting in the mid-morning sun, I clocked three figures shouldering television cameras, Lego-sized people in the distance. *Shit, this ain't a 'short walk' – more the length of Loughton High Street.* Or so it looked to me, anyway. Then somebody shouted, 'Action,' and off I sauntered, trying to look cool, calm and sexy in my white House of CB bandage bikini, hoping the penis-shaped shisha-pipe burn on my right thigh (a recent injury) wasn't obvious beneath the make-up artist's work. My inner voice chanted, *Don't fall over, Georgia. Don't fuck this up. You* cannot *fuck this up.*

I continued along the beach, following another cameraman who'd popped up some ten metres ahead, pacing backwards to capture my debut on the set of *The Only Way is Ibiza: Part One* – the first of two special episodes in the semi-reality series *The Only Way is Essex* (*TOWIE*).

God, I was nervous. This moment was massive for me, even though, off-screen, I was part of the *TOWIE* family already. Growing up around Loughton, Essex, one of the series's filming hotspots, I regularly socialised with the cast, some of whom had gone to the same schools as me. I'd been a hardcore fan since it launched in 2010. I thought the faces of *TOWIE* had it made. They were all living the life, getting paid to go out partying and making a living simply by being themselves; it seemed like a fun work–life balance to me. Landing a role on the show was a dream come true – my natural calling, surely? I tried to remember this as I walked towards the set, but seriously, my mouth felt like a lizard's arse on a hot summer's day. This was my first television shoot, and I was going in blind and alone. *How will I even get my words out?*

Although *TOWIE* is unscripted, I had inadvertently created a storyline. A few weeks back, while working as a shot girl in Marbella, I'd snogged cast member Lew (Lewis) Bloor in a nightclub, which wasn't an unusual event. Lew and I had kissed several times before – we'd flirted on and off with each other for the last three years, although we'd never actually got together or anything.

Recently, Lewis had been in a relationship with fellow *TOWIE* star Lauren Pope, but just before we kissed in Marbella, he said their romance had fizzled out (I'd subsequently learned otherwise). 'I haven't seen Lauren in weeks. I only came to Marbs to see you, babe,' he'd shouted in my ear above the throbbing house music. Then, bang, we were kissing. It was just a cheeky, drunken smooch. As I said, Lew and I had been here before, and I honestly didn't give our latest clinch too much thought – until a show producer called me, saying, 'We want you to come to Ibiza to appear in the next series of *TOWIE*. Are you up for it?'

In my head I was like, *Pour me a piña colada – I'm on the next flight.* There was no need to ask me twice: it was a definite 'yes' from me.

Relief washed over me when I finally reached the two girls, both in glam chiffony beachwear with gorgeous honey-highlighted hair tumbling past their shoulders.

The girl closest to me was my good mate, Georgia Kousoulou, who was a big-sister figure to me. Back home we were known as the 'two Gees'. She used to lend me her ID to get into clubs in my earlier teens. Georgia's a lovely girl, and I can't tell you how grateful I was to be sharing my first *TOWIE* scene with her.

I pattered over, kissed Georgia on both cheeks, and she was like, 'Oh. My. God. What are you doing here?' I'd been under strict lockdown in my hotel room since arriving in

15

Ibiza, so my sudden appearance was a surprise. She was with Lydia Bright, who I knew from the show but hadn't met until now. Georgia introduced me to her co-star, and I sat down on the empty sunbed beside them.

Watching this clip today, I can't help but laugh at myself. If you haven't seen it, this is what happens: after telling the girls I've been on the island for 'about two days', my attention quickly turns to the loaded drinks bucket to my right. 'Mind if I have a beer?' I ask, and Georgia replies, 'Yeah, go on'. I grab a bottle, shove it in my mouth and crack off its metal cap with my teeth.

Georgia snorts into her platinum-manicured hands, saying, 'Oh my God' again, clearly not expecting me to perform my party trick on camera, a stunt I'd earlier bigged up to the crew, hoping it'd give me a unique edge (it was long before I got my composites done!).

Anyway, a couple of swigs of Dutch courage later, I tell the girls about my night in Marbella with Lew and a few friends. 'He [Lewis] came out there [to Marbella]. He said he hadn't been with Lauren for about three weeks. Well, we all went out for dinner, we all got a bit drunk, and I snogged him . . .'

Georgia and Lydia exchange confused looks. 'What, wait a minute, he's with Lauren,' they say in unison, and I have no time to think. All I can do is tell the truth. 'He said he'd hardly spoken to Lauren,' I say, 'he said there's no spark between them and, honestly, I thought he would have gone home and broken it off with her.'

Then the camera zooms in on Georgia's face, her grimace

audible through dazzling clenched teeth before the scene fades to the sound of Gorgon City's 'Imagination'.

My debut in the can, I went straight back into hiding. If other cast members got wind of my presence, on or off set, I could be dropped from the show. 'We'll call you just before you're needed on set again,' a producer told me. So, I spent the rest of the day – and night – in my hotel room, doing sit-ups on the balcony, waiting for the phone to ring. I had a serious case of FOMO, knowing the rest of the cast were probably out filming and partying. But I did as I was told and stayed put – no way would I jeopardise this opportunity.

I shot my second *TOWIE* scene the following afternoon. My instructions were to enter a nightclub, which involved descending a flight of glass stairs in five-inch heels. Feeling a hundred times more nervous this time, I necked a glass of wine before I tackled those steps, which led me onto the dancefloor and directly to Lew.

He was with Lauren and Tommy Mallet, another cast newbie, when I teetered over. As I threw my arms around Lew's neck, I spotted Lauren Pope behind him, chatting with Lydia and Vas Morgan. Camera in my face, I told Lew straight: 'Look, I don't want to be the girl who kissed Lauren's boyfriend in Marbella – and that's sort of what I think that I am. I don't want to rub it in her face. You need to understand that.' Again, I was telling the truth; the last thing I wanted was for Lauren to think I'd deliberately muscled in on her boy – I would never do that.

'You don't have to feel bad,' was Lew's response. 'I kissed

you and you stopped it. I'm single now and that's all that matters.' That brief exchange concluded my second scene.

At nineteen, I was then one of the youngest actors on *TOWIE*. Suddenly, I found myself in the public eye. My Instagram account swelled from a few hundred followers to almost 70,000. I became an influencer, promoting products including hair extensions and make-up for beauty brands. It was ridiculous the amount of stuff I got for free.

Getting papped when out with my *TOWIE* co-stars was another new thing for me – although I was nowhere near a household name compared with the likes of Joey Essex or Gemma Collins. Fans constantly approached them for photo opportunities, so I felt chuffed whenever somebody asked to pose for pictures with me. My *TOWIE* role meant the world to me; it was a dream that had been a long time coming.

From the age of five, I aspired to become an actress. 'Georgia was a proper little entertainer when she was little – she still is,' says Mum, and I guess she's right. I've always enjoyed being in the spotlight, if only to make people laugh.

While I struggled with some subjects at school, I excelled at music and drama, and often landed the lead roles in school plays. Once, aged around nine or ten, I played Ariel in Shakespeare's *The Tempest*. That was a big number; I had to sing and play the flute, and I remember getting a massive round of applause and brilliant feedback after the show. My teachers told Mum, 'Georgia should definitely be an actress when she's older. She was fabulous out there.' Ah, Mum's eyes welled with pride. Even today, she loves flicking through the photographs of me as Ariel – she reckons I looked proper angelic in my ivory costume complete with sparkly wings. That was one of my finest moments at Chigwell School – before I got kicked out for 'misbehaving'.

Personally, I don't think I did much to warrant my expulsion, besides being a bit of a class clown. A page I created on Piczo (an early social-media and blogging platform) caused a stir, I recall.

On my page, which I designed during an IT lesson, I posted two photos I'd found online – one depicting a man with the world's biggest moobs and another showing a huge set of human testicles squished into a jar (I think this came from a joke world records site). Those images were accidentally broadcast on a big screen in the IT department to horrified parents and prospective pupils attending a new-intake open evening – the biggest annual event for the fee-paying school. I was in the classroom when it happened, acting as a pupil ambassador. Talk about a hear-a-pin-drop moment. A deathly silence filled the room, broken by the tip-tapping of keys as my classmate Matt hurriedly tried to erase the images accompanied by bold text screaming: *Check out the world's biggest balls and man-boobs.*

My parents got hauled in to see the headmistress – Dad said he couldn't stop laughing throughout the entire meeting. Then, about a week later, I got accused of throwing a rock at a car on a school scouting trip. It was a marshmallow, not a rock, but nevertheless, that minor incident was the straw that broke the camel's back for my headmistress. Then it was a fresh start for me at Roding Valley High School.

I was a bit of a lost soul during my secondary school years. Granted, I was quite naughty, mucking about in class, but I lacked confidence and focus. I suffered from acute psoriasis – my face, arms, legs and scalp were covered with red, flaky splodges. Horrible bullies nicknamed me 'Scabby' or 'Crusty', which made me feel ugly and worthless, despite my ability to stand up for myself. Gratefully, away from the handful of bullies, my brilliant circle of friends – Cenk, Reiss (who introduced me to Cenk), Bella, Rachel, Benj and sisters Tyla and Star – had my back no matter what. They'll be my best friends forever.

When I left school in summer 2011, armed with a handful of GCSEs, my acting dream seemed too far out of reach. I didn't have the right qualifications, experience or money to go to drama school, and my ancient Ariel performance would hardly cut it in the competitive world of stage and television. I panicked about my future and stressed about my past when I should've been embracing the present. Then, just after I turned seventeen, Tyla gave me a gift that would completely transform my outlook on the universe. 'You should read this,' said Tyla, handing me a copy of *The Secret*, a bestselling self-help book by Rhonda Byrne. 'It teaches you how to manifest your thoughts and dreams, using the laws of attraction to change your life path. Seriously, it's wicked.'

Wow, I devoured *The Secret*, hooked and moved by its introduction alone, which describes using 'The Secret' to learn who you truly are and achieve anything you want.

In *The Secret*, Byrne champions a three-step process to 'manifest' your desires. The first step is to 'ask' for what you want to achieve, be it a new job, wealth, a happy relationship or whatever, but once you've made your decisions, you must then 'believe' in them. The final step is to visualise and feel good about 'receiving' your desires. Being grateful for everything is key to finding joy and happiness, which will further enable you to manifest whatever you dream of, says Byrne.

The Secret blew me away. Buoyed by newfound positive energy, I started a manifestation journal, charting my aspirations and everything I was grateful for. My first manifestation list went like this:

1 – Get a part on *TOWIE*
2 – Become an influencer (so I don't have to pay for things)
3 – Get a French Bulldog
4 – Buy my own flat

Of course, those dreams wouldn't come true overnight. It took me two years to manifest *TOWIE*, and a lot of that manifesting happened in my subconscious mind, while I was doing other things.

Around that time, I juggled multiple jobs. I didn't care what I did or how many hours I worked, so long as I made money and mingled with people. A promotional agency I signed with booked me for some mad jobs. Once, I was a 'sausage girl' at Stamford Bridge stadium, which involved wearing a big placard around my neck while parading in front of a hot-dog stand in a plume of oniony smoke, shouting, 'Come and get your hot sausages'.

That slogan prompted the same line from most blokes. 'Oi, love, I've got a hot sausage for you,' they'd leer, and I'd respond with an oversized smile, thinking, *Yeah, really smart, mate – not heard that one before.*

Another job saw me in a yellow boiler suit, handing out vodka shots at a *Breaking Bad*-themed event at London's Shoreditch House. Waitressing gigs were the best. Easy work, really; all I had to do was rock up at posh venues like the Shard and serve canapés and champagne to VIPs. Some girls I worked with moaned about their aching legs and feet, which I understood – it was tiring work – but I loved it. I got stuck into the canapés and champagne. *I'm not working, I'm just part of the party. Bring it on,* I thought. I'd be the tipsiest waitress, but the agency kept rebooking me after clients raved about my 'chirpy' demeanour.

I threw myself into every job I did, determined to enjoy the moment. Alongside my promo shifts I also worked nights, shot-girling in clubs. During my breaks I kept writing my manifestations, my *TOWIE* wish constantly topping those lists.

The manifestation process is a powerful phenomenon, but, as I've learned over the years, you need to enjoy and own your successes. Sometimes, you can manifest a dream situation, only to be overwhelmed with imposter syndrome once it happens. Although I manifested my *TOWIE* role, I didn't embrace that opportunity with the same confidence I have today. Negative thoughts plagued my mind: *I'm not good enough. I don't deserve to be here. Why am I not getting more scenes?*

I kind of felt like a spare part on *TOWIE*. The pay wasn't great initially – around £150 a day – and I couldn't do other work because I was on standby for filming twenty-four-seven. But, like many of my castmates, I clung to the honour of being on the show.

Most weeks I only worked on Wednesdays and Sundays (the main filming days). My storylines, devoid of major rows, tears and tantrums, didn't venture beyond the will-they-won't-they? scenario with Lew and a short-lived romance with another castmate, Tom Pearce, so I guess I couldn't expect to film every day. Network bosses wanted high drama to keep the million-plus viewers on the edges of their seats, right?

I won't lie. I struggled to get involved with the social dynamics on set. Everyone else seemed established and naturally confident, whereas I needed a couple of drinks to be myself on camera. Instead of being my authentic self, I worried about not being a big enough character. I did get excited about filming my first *TOWIE* Christmas event though.

'The theme is a "festive" party,' said the director.

Ah, how lovely, I thought, *I'm gonna nail this one*. Mum and I traipsed around Westfield shopping centre for hours looking for an outfit. We finally decided on a cute Rudolph affair, comprising an arse-skimming fawn velvet dress, a flashing red nose and a headpiece sprouting ears and antlers.

'Oh, that's made for you, sweetie,' said Mum, snapping pictures of me in my reindeer gear before I left for the shoot.

'Ah, thank you,' I said, striking a few red carpet-inspired poses, antlers bobbing as I laughed and drained a glass of white. 'You watch, the whole *TOWIE* cast will be dashing out to buy reindeer outfits tomorrow.'

Turned out, nobody asked me where I'd bought my Rudolph get-up. The second I pranced into the filming venue, a mansion in the Essex countryside, my fake ears and antlers wilted with embarrassment. All the other girls were in slinky, jewel-encrusted ballgowns. I'm talking *Hello!* glamour to my Christmas-catalogue look. The whole room cracked up. Even the walls and chandeliers laughed at me, I swear. *Fuck, how did I misread the brief?* I laughed with my colleagues, novelty laughter that complemented my outfit but masked my devastation. What else could I do?

The next morning, Mum burst into my bedroom brandishing a newspaper. 'Look, Georgia, you've had the last laugh.' I sat up in bed, blinking as Mum passed me the tabloid – the *Sun*, I think. Anyway, there I was on the page, looking a little worse for wear in my comedy costume, antlers skew-whiff, a reindeer ear flopped over my left eye. 'Ear Comes George,' declared the headline. It was a great article, capturing my true self. Mum and I proper belly laughed for ages. *I'm going to up my game now*, I thought. *I will make it big on* TOWIE.

The universe had other ideas.

I'd just stepped outside the ITV studios on London's South Bank when a *TOWIE* executive called me. 'Stay where you are, George,' he said, 'we've sent a taxi for you – we need you to come into the office for a chat.'

'Okay, great, see you soon,' I breezed, buzzing after my first live appearance on daytime television to promote a charity fundraising event for *TOWIE*. Waiting in the foyer, I took my manifestation journal out of my bag and wrote a new list, titled 'Career and Work':

1 – I want to get my own ITV show.
2 – I want to become a presenter.
3 – I want to go on *I'm a Celebrity ... Get Me Out of Here!*
4 – I want to have one million Instagram followers in the next six months.
5 – I want to land a fashion collab with a huge brand.

I continued writing during the taxi ride to Lime Pictures's offices, relatively unfazed about the upcoming meeting. This was my first visit to the office and, naively, I assumed other *TOWIE* stars would also be at this 'chat'. *It's probably a group briefing about filming or something*, I thought as we pulled up outside a converted warehouse tucked away down a backstreet in Fitzrovia. I sashayed through the glass doors all smiles. 'Hiya, I'm Georgia Harrison,' I told the receptionist. 'I'm here for the *TOWIE* meeting.'

What happened next is still fuzzy in my mind. I remember sitting in a white open-plan office with two production bosses whose names and faces escape me. Those two blokes turned to watery blobs before me the moment they started talking, when the words 'we're sorry' crashed through my heart like a freight train at full pelt.

'We don't need you on *TOWIE* anymore,' continued one of the guys.

'So, you're dropping me?' I asked – the only words I could muster without having a massive meltdown.

'We might look into having you back in the future but, for now . . . '

I didn't catch the rest of that sentence. In my head it was game over, my *TOWIE* dream shattered. I managed a meek, 'Thank you for having me,' before I left. I sobbed all the way home to Essex.

Mum was annoyed at the abruptness of my sacking. 'Bloody hell, Georgia,' she said, 'I mean, they could've warned you – I would've come with you to that meeting. No way should you have gone through that alone.'

God, I was devastated. Mostly, I dreaded what my ex-co-stars thought of me. *Am I the first* TOWIE *actor to be dumped after only one series?* I moped around in my pyjamas for a couple of days, crying on and off, believing my television career was over. But then a switch flicked inside of me. I thought, *Sod it, you're made of tougher stuff than this. Turn this experience into something positive.*

In hindsight, I understand why I got fired from *TOWIE*. First, I wasn't seeing anyone at the time (Tom Pearce had dumped me in one of my last scenes), and secondly, I was probably a bit immature on set.

I dusted off my copy of *The Secret*, ready for a new start. Before, I'd thought *TOWIE* was my be-all and end-all. Now I viewed my reality-TV stint as a stepping stone to further opportunities.

Making money was my priority, so I joined a temping agency, happy to take on any roles that came my way, my mantra being, *Nothing is above or below me*. A few days after submitting my (slightly embellished) CV to the agency, I started work on a construction site bordering a sewage plant in Barkingside. Hired as an admin clerk, I was the only woman on site, based in a portable office overlooking the sewage works. I had to wear a high-vis jacket, a hard hat and donkey boots and, no exaggeration, every square inch of the place, inside and out, reeked of ripe shit. I remember Mum crying when she dropped me there one morning – usually I'd take two buses to the site but there was a strike on that day. 'I don't want to leave you here,' she wept, the stench of human faeces wafting through the car's air vents.

I gave Mum a reassuring peck on the cheek. 'Honestly, it's fine, Mum.' And off I went to tackle more spreadsheets. Okay, working on a construction site next to a shit plant hadn't featured on my manifestation list but, smell aside,

I was grateful to have a job. Career-wise, being on my arse fuelled my spiritual development. I filled multiple journals with daily affirmations, my faith in the universe growing stronger by the day.

Three weeks later I said cheerio to the boys at the construction site to start another temp job, followed by several more. Then, in early 2016, I became a personal assistant to the CEO of a City financial consultancy firm. Again, this was only supposed to be a short-term contract, but I ended up staying with the company for well over a year. I felt valued at work; my boss, JD, was such an inspirational character. He ran regular resilience training classes for staff, his catchphrase being: 'You can do *anything*.' Without a doubt, JD gave me the confidence to be the person I am today. 'You're a powerful force in this office, Georgia,' he frequently told me. 'You light up the room, just by being here.'

Meanwhile, my personal life was also going well. I'd rekindled my romance with Jake McLean, and we were now practically living together in my new rented flat in Debden, Essex. We rarely spent a night apart. We fell into a normal routine of going to work, eating breakfast and dinner together, having sex and snuggling up in front of the telly on my crushed-velvet sofa (crushed-velvet furniture was all the rage in Essex then). We lived like this for nine months before things nosedived. Jake announced he had to move abroad for work. I was heartbroken, as was Jake, but we didn't split up as such. We agreed to keep in touch long-distance, but I knew things couldn't stay the same. *How can we be together if we can barely see each other?*

Despite Jake being a lads' lad, I loved him with all my heart. He always wanted me to shine. Soon after he moved away, I got signed by Neil Dobias, agent and manager at Force 1 Management. I was over the moon at the prospect of reigniting my TV career – and Neil reckoned he could get me on the nation's favourite reality show. 'I've spoken with the people at *Love Island,* and I think you should apply,' he said over drinks one night. 'You're just what they're looking for – you'll be great.'

Naturally, I was thrilled to hear this. Much as I enjoyed my job, I couldn't see myself staying there forever, commuting back and forth to London's Liverpool Street, and being stuck within the same four walls every day. As my journals attested, I desperately wanted to get back into television, but *Love Island?* I hoped to work things out with Jake. How would he react to me mincing about in a bikini and getting it on with ripped boys on national television? Part of me was still deeply disappointed that Jake had taken a job abroad, but I couldn't hurt his feelings. That's how much I loved him.

So, I told Neil, 'Look, I really appreciate the offer, but, as you know, I've got a boyfriend. I'm settled with Jake – I can't do this to him.'

Neil's eyes disappeared into his forehead for a second. 'Oh, I know what Jake's like – he's known for being a bit of a one with the ladies. Just fill in the application form, see what happens. If you get the job, you can always turn it down.'

'Okay,' I said. 'But I'll need to run it by Jake first.'

I called Jake later that night after a few Sauvignon Blancs. 'They want me to go on *Love Island*,' I blurted. I was so nervous, I sounded like I'd been on the helium balloons.

'Well, you need to do it then, George. I'm going to be away from home for a long time. I don't want you to waste the best years of your life waiting for me to come back,' was Jake's calm response.

'Seriously, you don't mind?'

'No, I want you to have this opportunity. I can just see you on the front pages of newspapers and magazines. Your personality is so special, Georgia – people need to see that. I'm not going to speak to you until you've done this – I'm not going to hold you back.'

I welled up then. 'I love you, Jake.'

'I love you too, Georgia.'

'I'll try,' I said, 'but please don't cut me off. You don't need to do that.' Still, we agreed to park our relationship for the time being. I was gutted but, deep down, I knew Jake was right. If I were to be chosen for *Love Island*, it could open new doors for me. I resolved to give it a shot, but I couldn't get Jake out of my head. I bombarded him with daily WhatsApp messages. *Please, Jake, speak to me*, I wrote. *I miss your voice so much*. He'd read my messages – two blue ticks at the bottom of my rambling texts confirmed as much – but he didn't reply to a single one of them.

*

It's sod's law, isn't it – the opportunities you're not overly fussed about are invariably the ones that land in your lap. In spring 2017, I got called into the ITV2 offices to audition for *Love Island*.

The interview was on a weekday afternoon, so I had to concoct an excuse to escape the office. I told JD I had an appointment to view a venue for an upcoming staff talent evening I'd been asked to arrange. He didn't bat an eye.

I went into that interview calm as you like, thinking, *If I don't get it, it's because I'm meant to be with Jake.* At least twenty other girls were auditioning that day, all of them in heels and bodycon dresses. Perfect hair and make-up. I was wearing jeans, trainers and a little shirt tied at my midriff. Once upon a time, I dreaded being the only underdressed woman in the room. Today, however, I really didn't give a shit. I was happy being myself.

We girls were left to chat for a while around a board-room table. Knowing the executive producers in the room were secretly observing us, I got stuck in, told some funny stories, cracked a few jokes. I was showing off, but somebody's gotta get the party started, don't they?

Next came our individual interviews, held in an adjacent room before a panel of show execs and television cameras. I didn't shut up in there. Asked about my dating history, I pulled all manner of outlandish stories out of my arse. 'I'm just back from a ski trip,' I lied, 'I had a mad one-night stand with a French boy. God, he was fit. I'm up for anything, me. I'm single and ready to mingle.' Well, I couldn't exactly sit there crying my eyes out, saying, 'I was with a boy for nine months, but I haven't been with anyone since – please can I have a tissue?'

My act worked; the producers recruited me for the third series of *Love Island*, but as a potential 'bombshell' rather than an original contestant, meaning, at some stage during the show, I might enter the *Love Island* villa in Mallorca, my intended role being to ruffle some feathers among existing couples. Or even steal another girl's partner. 'We'll give you twenty-four hours' notice if you're needed,' were the producers' parting words. Then, radio silence.

Honestly, I thought I'd never appear on *Love Island*. My bags, packed with shedloads of gear, sat sheepishly in my living room for over three weeks before I finally got the call saying, 'You're going into the villa – you're flying out at 5 p.m. today.' Although sworn to secrecy, I told a handful of trusted people about my imminent *Love Island* appearance, namely Mum, Jake (in another message that prompted blue ticks but no reply), Cenk, my best girlfriends and JD, who was thrilled for me. 'Go for it, Georgia,' he said on my final day in the office, 'I've got every faith in you.' Then, with a fleeting serious look, he added, 'By the way, would you mind deleting your LinkedIn page before you leave? We don't really want the company associated with *Love Island* . . . just in case.'

I laughed, hugged my boss and workmates goodbye, then headed to the airport. Just before I boarded the plane to Mallorca, Jake messaged me: *I believe in you, Georgia. Smash it – you've got this.* A tear trickled down my face, emotions brewing inside of me, a mixture of nerves and loss – but also excitement. *He's setting me free to pursue my dreams.* That's what I told myself, anyway.

Wearing a postbox-red bodycon dress, I entered the *Love Island* villa on day thirty-four of the series. Typically, the other girls were head-to-toe in white. 'I must not have got the memo,' I joked as I advanced across the decking in my heels towards my fellow contestants. My feelings for Jake notwithstanding, I'd decided to go into this experience with a relaxed, *que-sera-sera* mindset. But my first task on *Love Island* was tough. I had to pick a boy to 'couple-up' with. That put me in an awkward spot; I'd stopped watching the series at home, thinking my 'bombshell' moment wouldn't materialise. That meant I wasn't up to speed on the latest *Love Island* gossip. I had no choice though; I had to pick somebody, so I went for Kem Cetinay, because he seemed a sound bloke: friendly, good banter – the type I would normally go for at home. Obviously, I wouldn't have picked Kem if I'd known he and Amber Davies were a couple. Yeah, that sparked fireworks. When I tried to apologise to Amber, she waggled her finger in my face, eyes blazing. 'Don't speak to me, you're fucking rude,' she raged. 'If anyone's a bellend, it's you, babe. You picked my boyfriend. He's *my* boyfriend.'

If you watched the series, you'll remember I broke down during a confessional following my showdown with Amber. I didn't want to cry on television, but I felt better for it afterwards. As I said to the camera, 'I'm not going to hit on Kem.' I kept to my word and, once the dust had settled, Amber and I got along fine.

I really enjoyed my time on *Love Island*. I got together with Geordie boy Sam Gowland, which was good fun while it lasted. Away from the 'coupling' pressure, the atmosphere was refreshingly relaxing. There were no clocks in the villa – or on our mobile phones, which were set to gallery mode. It was nice to chill out, get to know new people and not think about the time. I'd lost count of the days when the public voted Sam and me off the show, just one week before the finale. But I was happy to leave – I'd had a wicked time.

Love Island entirely changed my life. My Instagram following skyrocketed to over a million, just as I'd wished for, which gave me the platform I have today to help other people.

Gradually, more of my dreams became realities. When my landlord put my flat on the market, I had enough money in the bank for a deposit to buy it, which I did.

But what next after *Love Island*? Well, I desperately wanted to go on Channel 4's *Celebs Go Dating*, and Neil did get me an audition. However, that wasn't meant to be. Instead, I ended up on MTV's reality endurance show, *The Challenge* – alongside Stephen Bear, but I'll save that story for another chapter . . .

Looking back over my manifestation journals today, I realise how much I've learned. As a nineteen-year-old kid, I obsessed about being on *TOWIE*, only to not fully enjoy that dream when it came true. I now know I changed that manifestation – and attracted more opportunities in the process, simply by asking, believing and receiving. So, my advice to you, should you wish to take it, is this: every thought has a power. If you're going to aim, aim big – and when you get there, enjoy the moment. Own it. You've created it. You deserve it.

'HAVE FAITH IN
THE TIMING OF THE
UNIVERSE. YOU
WILL NEVER MISS
OUT ON ANYTHING
THAT IS TRULY
DESTINED FOR YOU.'

'MAYBE IT WASN'T SUPPOSED TO WORK OUT. MAYBE IT'S SUPPOSED TO END TO MAKE ROOM FOR SOMETHING BETTER, SOMETHING KINDER, SOMETHING SO GOOD YOU WON'T EVER HAVE TO QUESTION IT.'

Chapter Two

TAKING BACK
MY RELATIONSHIPS

'I've had bags of crisps that have lasted longer than my relationships,' I always tell my friends. It's my habitual one-liner, delivered with a laugh, sigh or mascara-infused tears. Sounds a bit sad, I know, but I hope to eradicate this saying from my vocab soon.

Most of my relationships have been short-term affairs. In the past, I'd fallen for bad boys or narcissists who initially swept me off my feet – then left me broken-hearted. I've endured toxic and abusive relationships but, equally, some partners have treated me with love and respect, even though those relationships didn't survive the test of time.

My parents separated soon after my second birthday. I don't remember the day Dad left home – I was too young; he moved abroad and started another family with a new partner, so he wasn't around as much as my friends' fathers were when I was growing up. Don't get me wrong, I love Dad dearly – he's the best dad in the world who's supported me through thick and thin. Since splitting from Mum, he's always done his best to see me as often as possible, but as a child, his absence from home sometimes made me feel unwanted – though I now know this wasn't his, or Mum's, fault. Back then, they struggled to hide family issues from me, so I often felt stuck in the middle of a negative co-parenting situation, which left me feeling hurt and confused at times. On the plus side, I went from being an only child to gaining my stepmum, Leigh, and three amazing half-siblings – Darcey; her younger brother, Danny; and his twin sister, Eva. Nowadays, I love having a second family.

Since embarking on a healing journey – and noticing patterns in my adult relationships – I recognise that some negative feelings I held as a young girl may have impacted how I approach relationships. I'd shy away from men who did want to commit to me, gravitating instead towards those who were there but not truly invested in the relationship. It's almost like I didn't expect a boyfriend to show up for me.

That said, I've never had trouble forming solid relationships with my male friends. As a little girl, I wasn't interested in dollies or cuddly toys. Being a proper tomboy, I preferred playing video games, runouts and building treehouses with the boys. I cherish these platonic relationships. If only my romantic endeavours were as simple. One of my first serious relationships remains vivid in my mind today . . .

I was in my late teens when I became involved with Shane. I met him via a mutual friend, and initially, we got along great. I fancied Shane. There was chemistry between us, I thought. He seemed really keen; he called and messaged and complimented me loads, and I felt flattered at first, especially as I lacked confidence then. But weeks into our relationship, the attentive Shane I'd come to love and trust transformed into an extremely insecure and troubled individual who abused me mentally and physically.

Before I go on, can I just say that I don't wish to give Shane much airtime here – because I believe he did truly love me, despite his issues. My only reason for sharing this dark chapter in my life is to hopefully reach out to other women who have suffered – or are still suffering – at the hands of abusive partners.

Shane's aggression towards me started with verbal abuse. He criticised my appearance, which really hurt me. Once, immediately after we'd had sex, he shot me this foul look: eyes scanning every inch of my naked body. Lips sucked in, cheeks ballooning with air as though he were about to vomit over the bed. 'What? What's wrong?' I asked.

Shane swung his chin from side to side in slow motion. 'You're fat,' he replied. 'You might look all right when you're dressed, but with your clothes off, you're disgusting.'

I lay there silently, eyes swimming, thinking, *I'm the ugliest girl in the world. I'm fat. Shane thinks I'm disgusting.* I was barely a size ten but, from the moment the word 'fat' left his lips, I convinced myself I was overweight.

Shane repeatedly accused me of cheating on him. He'd

steal my mobile phone, then lock me out of the room while he scrolled through my messages, searching for non-existent 'evidence'. Twice, Shane smashed my phone to bits. Another time, just after we'd left a restaurant, he spat in my face. 'You were giving that waiter provocative looks – and don't deny it,' he growled.

I lived in a perpetual state of fear, terrified of what I might say or do next to set him off. He made me hate myself – to the extent I began to believe I *deserved* his degrading comments and aggression. I didn't, and thankfully, I realised this, albeit several months down the line, when I finally ended our relationship.

Still, it took me a while to regain my confidence. Shane's vicious remarks about my looks stuck with me; some days, I couldn't bring myself to look in the mirror. In my head I thought, *Will I ever again appreciate this body God has given me? Will the next man I'm with also think I'm disgusting?* Jake was the first man who truly made me feel beautiful and confident as a woman.

Ah, Jake. Where do I begin? I'm crying already, picturing his smile, sunnier than Ibiza. The beauty spot beneath his left eye that twitched when he laughed. I remember resting my head on his bare shoulder and getting lost in the swirls of ink covering his chest and arms (I do love a man with tattoos).

I knew Jake and I would become more than friends from the second he came into my life almost twelve years ago. Of all places, I first met him in my mate Owen's car on the way home from a party. The attraction was mutual, our banter palpably flirtatious from the get-go. His laugh boomed above the car stereo. I'll never forget Jake's infectious laugh.

After that night, Jake became part of my social circle. In my late teens I spent a lot of time at his flat, which he shared with his cousin Kane. We'd watch TV and chat and laugh until we cried. Sometimes, we'd end up kissing, but we didn't take things further until much later.

I adored Jake's sense of humour and pretty-boy looks that belied his laddish reputation.

In late 2016, Jake and I finally became a couple. We had a playful partnership; we loved winding each other up, in a jokey way, and randomly dancing around the kitchen together late at night. Jake was a proper romantic at heart, too. He used to play our song, 'Perfect' by Ed Sheeran, in the car, cranking up the volume as we both sang along. I remember our 'silly part' – where Jake and I would howl like wolves as Ed echoed the word 'home'. Jake had a stunning singing voice. I used to tell him, 'You should audition for *The X Factor* or *Britain's Got Talent*.' He'd laugh off my suggestions. That was Jake through and through. He didn't take himself or life too seriously.

Like the title of our song, my life with Jake felt perfect. I couldn't imagine myself with anyone else but him. We'd even discussed the possibility of having kids together in the future. 'If I'm going to have a baby with anyone, it'll be with you, George,' Jake said in bed one night.

On my daily commute to my job in the City, I'd write in my journal, 'I'm grateful for the love Jake gives to me,' thinking, *How bloody lucky am I?* Or, 'Thank you, Jake, for giving me the confidence to love myself,' and so on, filling pages and pages with my words of gratitude for 'the best boyfriend ever'.

I could never have imagined the heartache ahead . . .

Jake picked a Sunday morning to drop his bombshell. He shambled solemnly into the living room, turned off the TV and sat beside me on the sofa. He slumped forward, face in his hands.

'Oh my God, are you okay, babe?' I said, giving his thigh a little rub.

Jake dropped his hands into his lap and turned to face me. For a moment I wondered whether this was one of his pranks, half expecting him to poke me in the ribs and say, 'Gotcha.' I wanted to hear his big laugh. Instead, I heard eight words that ripped my world apart: 'I'm sorry. I need to tell you something.'

Jake spilled before I could reply. 'I'm moving abroad, for work. I want to stay with you but I can't see how it will work – I'll be thousands of miles away. I love you so much though George, believe me.'

'No, what the fuck?' Now I was the one covering my face, crying and crying and crying. 'I can't believe this is happening.'

'I'm so sorry, Georgia. Tell me what to do. I'll do anything.'

I lifted my head and the room swayed. 'How could you let this happen to us?' I choked. My world shattered in that moment.

'Hopefully I won't be away forever, and you could—'

'Look, Jake, I can't cope with this right now,' I said. 'Just take me to my mum's. I'm in no fit state to drive.'

Neither of us spoke in the car, both silently smoking cigarettes. We stopped a short distance away from Mum's house, and Jake switched off the engine. My heart died with it.

'Is this it? Am I gonna lose you?' he asked.

'I don't know, Jake, I don't know if we can get past this.' I couldn't think straight. I was too angry, too upset, too confused. Everything we had grown to love was broken beyond repair. How could we continue our relationship if we weren't even living in the same country? 'I mean, for fuck's sake, Jake, last night we were figuring out what to have for dinner – and now . . . this?'

Jake reached for my hand and apologised again. 'I actually love you so much, George. You're not like all the other girls. You're different, special. I hope you know that?'

I half nodded, mumbled something about needing some headspace, then got out of the car, devastated.

When I returned after filming *Love Island*, Jake was still living abroad. Although we'd both moved on with our lives – and accepted we were no longer an 'item' – we still called each other and exchanged flirty messages most days. He also gave me great fashion advice, updating me on the latest trends, which came in handy when I was asked to launch my own collection of 'trendy streetwear' for fashion brand Lasula.

In the wake of *Love Island* and my brief relationship

with fellow contestant Sam Gowland, I was happy to be single and stepping up my fitness regime before competing in MTV's reality show, *The Challenge: War of the Worlds*, which was due to start filming in October 2018.

In the fifteen months leading up to *The Challenge*, Jake and I continued our relationship on and off following his surprise return to Essex. I worked on my manifestations, creating new lists alongside revisiting my old journals. Looking at my first list from 2011, I crossed off wish number three: 'Get a French Bulldog'. I now had Sky, a beautiful blue-coated French Bulldog, kindly gifted to me by a friend of a friend whose pet had given birth to a litter of puppies.

I'd just left my flat with Sky one afternoon when Stephen Bear bowled up in a Mercedes SUV. I recognised him instantly when he zipped down the window: that cocky grin and year-round sunbed tan, 'Be the Best' inked down the left side of his neck. His number plate, 'B19 BEAR', was also a giveaway. He gave me a tattooed wave, and said something like, 'You all right, Georgia? What are you doing here?' I knew Bear from the reality-TV circuit, but we'd only exchanged quick hellos at parties.

I crouched beside Bear's car, trying to attach the lead to Sky's collar as she jumped and yapped. She was desperate for a wee, bless her. 'I live here,' I said. 'That's my flat over there.' I motioned over my shoulder, conscious of my terrible post-photoshoot make-up – zombie-like charcoal eyeliner and foundation that cracked when I smiled. 'What're you doing down here, anyway?'

Bear pushed his shades into his gelled hair and side-nodded at the end-of-terrace house bang opposite my flat. 'I've just bought that house, so I guess I'll be seeing you around.'

'Yeah, I guess you will,' I said, then hurried away with Sky before she relieved herself against Bear's shiny Merc.

Regrets?

Weirdly, I next bumped into Bear two weeks later at London Heathrow Airport, along with former footballer Ashley Cain, Theo Campbell, my good mate from *Love Island*, and a small production crew.

I'd read in the press about potential other contestants but hadn't paid much attention to the rumours. Now, here I was with three of my Great Britain teammates, ready to go head-to-head with our counterparts from America and Brazil in *The Challenge: War of the Worlds*. *Geordie Shore* star Zahida Allen, would complete our squad, although she'd be travelling on a separate flight from me and the boys, explained one of the production guys, who then announced our destination: Namibia – in south-west Africa.

I got chatting to Bear in the security queue. 'I guess we'll be seeing even more of each other now,' I said.

'Yeah, I can't wait,' Bear replied in his husky voice. He was wearing a grey tracksuit that showed off his muscles and, I'll admit, I thought he looked hot. I texted Mum from the airport, before we handed our phones over to the production crew. 'You'll never guess what?' I typed. 'Stephen Bear's here – he's well fit.' I added a few bear and flexed biceps emojis. Mum was impressed; she'd loved watching Bear on *Celebrity Big Brother 2016*.

Hours later, after a few shots of Baileys from the in-flight drinks trolley, Bear and I were in high-speed flirtation mode. He was full of flattering comments, telling me I looked beautiful and fit and stuff. I played up to this, saying things like, 'You're proper naughty, Bear. A bit of a wrong 'un.' And so our banter continued throughout the flight.

Bear had strong energy and fast emerged as the entertainer in our team. Of course, I knew he was trouble. His past relationships had been splashed all over the press: I'd recently read about his romance with a model, but I'd heard reports that they'd since broken up. Bear confirmed as much when we touched down in Africa.

'I'm single now,' said Bear as I perched on his lap during our nocturnal coach ride into the Namibian desert.

I was so excited – we all were – especially when we arrived at our camp. It was such a magical vista: a white tent, surrounded by production lorries, nestled in the sand beneath the clear, star-studded desert sky. I wished my family and friends were there to share the moment.

We all stank after more than fifteen hours of travelling. None of us could freshen up or get changed until our luggage had been combed for contraband by security. Not that this bothered us; we were too busy getting to know our American and Brazilian competitors, who'd also found fame on reality-TV shows. At Bear's suggestion, that meet and greet soon escalated to a game of spin the bottle inside our tent. We acted like a bunch of twelve-year-olds on a sleepover rather than so-called 'titans' preparing for battle to win the $1 million prize. I was in my element.

The Challenge contest itself was murderous. Working in pairs, we faced a daily routine of gruelling physical and mental tasks to avoid elimination from the show. We cycled marathons in the desert heat, ran up and down vertical sand dunes chasing tumbling basketballs, got dragged through the baking sand while clinging to a tyre roped to a speeding monster truck, and had wrestling matches on the 'Killing Floor'.

On our second day in Namibia, we moved into *The Challenge* villa – a huge affair with eight bedrooms, an upstairs lounge with poker and pool tables, a gym and an outdoor swimming pool. There were crystals throughout the house, which added to the aura of love in the air. Rose quartz, the crystal of love, heavily bordered the swimming pool, glistening with the power of desire in the Namibian heat.

Bear and I grew closer by the day. Behind his gregarious facade I discovered a gentle, loving side to him – and I think this is an important part of my story to stress. We'd chat for hours while lounging by the pool. The other contestants said we looked like 'two loved-up, sunbathing beavers'. At that point, I trusted Bear.

The desert, naturally, was freezing at night, and I'd come ill-prepared for this drastic dip in temperature. Cenk, Bella and Reiss had helped me pack just a few hours before my flight (we'd been up drinking until four in the morning), so when I opened my case, I found it rammed with crop tops, shorts, bikinis, and little skirts and dresses. Bear laughed endearingly when he saw me shivering in a skimpy tutu dress while the others pulled on their tracksuits and jumpers. 'It's all right, Georgia, you can share my clothes,' he said, giving me a big hug that further won me over.

Thankfully, the cameras didn't capture my more intimate moments with Bear. As our relationship grew physical, we'd sneak into one of the bathrooms, remove our microphones and have quiet sex, knowing that there was no way the cameras could catch us in there. I didn't want my sex life broadcast to the world, and Bear respected that. He wasn't giving it the 'showman' act then – maybe because, unbeknown to me, he hadn't broken up with his girlfriend back home.

I was raging when I learned Bear had lied to me – a scene that was caught on camera but not aired live as *The Challenge* is pre-recorded.

Once every two weeks, as a treat, we were allowed to phone call a loved one from a private mini conference-style room. One such evening, about four weeks into filming, I overheard Bear on FaceTime to his 'cousin'. I wasn't the only one who witnessed it – he'd left the door wide open – and I just happened to be in the adjacent kitchen, toothbrush in one hand, glass of water in the other, when I heard a female voice speaking.

I pulled the toothbrush out of my mouth and tiptoed towards the doorway, catching the woman's stunning face on the wall-mounted screen above the back of Bear's head. Their chat told me she and Bear were much more than cousins.

'I miss you too,' she said. 'Is there anything I need to worry about?'

'Nah, why?' Bear replied from his armchair. He sounded nervous to me.

'You say, "I miss you a lot." I haven't heard from you in like . . . if there's anything, I'd rather you just tell me, and I don't have to—'

'Yeah, there's nothing to worry about,' Bear confirmed.

I marched into the room, certain whoever he was talking to must be his girlfriend. I mean, what the fuck? As I later said in a confessional: 'Did he really think he could be with me out here, sit there on the phone to her, and neither of us were gonna find out?'

When I confronted Bear, he insisted the woman I'd seen on the screen was his cousin – even though I'd heard her say, 'Is that Georgia?' towards the end of their conversation.

I called Bear into the kitchen to face me and our house-mates, branding him a 'two-faced lying scumbag'. 'Sorry I just disturbed you talking to the girlfriend that you told everyone you don't have,' I yelled, jabbing my toothbrush in the air. 'Are you gonna come out and face your issues? Or are you just gonna sit there looking at the wall?'

Out he came, avoiding my glare as he shuffled past, looking bored. 'That was my cousin on the phone,' he mumbled, then sat on top of one of the long tables.

I got right up in his face. 'How does your cousin know my name?'

'I don't know.'

I was livid – and that's an understatement. Earlier that day, Bear and I had cosied up in my bunk bed, kissing and cuddling. I reminded him of this as I fired more questions his way.

'That's my cousin, that's my cousin, that's my cousin, that's my cousin, that's my cousin,' was all I got out of him, by which point, I'd had enough of his bare-faced lies. 'That's my cousin, that's my cousin, that's my—'

I chucked my water at him, a great aim that soaked his hair then rained down his cheating face. 'Fucking prick,' I sneered. 'Don't ever come near me again.' I turned and left him dripping over the kitchen floor.

A few days after our row, Bear admitted, in a roundabout way, that he'd lied about his relationship status. 'Okay,' he said, 'I didn't split up with her as such. Before I came out here, things were on and off, and we kind of left things hanging in the air. But I promise you, she's definitely my ex now.'

Bear continued, his tone worryingly convincing as he reminded me of the good times we'd shared pre-FaceTimegate, 'Look, we've been together from the very beginning in here. We have cuddles and kisses and share secrets. If I lose you, I think I might as well go home. I really want to mend things with you, Georgia.'

In the end, I forgave Bear. Looking back, I think our surroundings influenced my decision. I mean, there we were, thirty-six randoms sharing a villa in the middle of the African desert. Apart from our weekly phone calls, we had no other external stimuli: no television, social media, magazines or newspapers. Human interaction keeps you sane in these circumstances. Plus, I'd missed hanging out with Bear. I missed him even more when he got eliminated from the series in week six. Although I didn't admit this to myself at the time, a part of me hoped Bear would want to rekindle our romance in the UK. But when I returned home two weeks later, proud to have finished eighth in *The Challenge*, Mum told me Bear's antics had made the papers again. 'His feet had barely touched the ground before he was photographed out with lots of other girls,' she said.

Although we were neighbours, Bear and I rarely bumped into one another at home in Essex, but we did rekindle our relationship for a short period in spring 2019 during a Muay Thai training camp, where we were joined by my *Love Island* mates Theo Campbell and Kaz Crossley. It wasn't planned; we just kind of picked up where we left off in Namibia. Once again, I fell for his charm. He seemed more mature, gentlemanly even. 'You're the only girl for me, Georgia,' he vowed.

After our holiday romance, I flew home and left him in Thailand. We remained friends, but led separate lives until I returned to Thailand to film *The Challenge: War of the Worlds 2* with him. Theo had also signed for the series. It felt like old times again: Team Great Britain was back and in it to win it.

Long story short, nobody in our team, which included a few new faces from the UK's reality-TV scene, reached the final, but I decided to stay in Chiang Mai for a break after filming.

Following my elimination in episode ten, I felt so sad and lost. Alone in Thailand, unsure whether my co-stars were still on the island, I sat in my dingy hotel room. I had no phone – the production team had confiscated it – so, one night, I wrote a letter to the universe. It went something like this: *God, I know you always have a plan, but I'm feeling so down right now. I don't know what to do or where to go. Please send me a sign and help guide me on this stage of my journey.*

The next morning, Sally, from *The Challenge* production team, came to my hotel room and returned my phone. She also delivered a surprising message: 'Bear is still here,' she whispered in my ear as I switched on my device. Hundreds of messages swamped my screen, but the most recent one filled me with joy: *Where are you, cuz?* The message was from my best friend and cousin, Sian. She had been travelling alone in Asia for the last four months. I knew she was heading through Thailand, but what were the odds of her being anywhere near me?

I responded, *Yo cuz, I've just come off* The Challenge, *I'm in Chiang Mai. My head's all over the place . . . Where are you?*

Waiting for her response, I uploaded a cheeky Insta story, letting everyone know I was in Thailand and, indirectly, that I was now off the show. Bear replied immediately. *Call me, I'm in Phuket. I want you to come here,* he said.

I didn't know what to think. *Bear's here? And he wants to meet? Can I really fly across the other side of Thailand and stay with him? I don't trust him to look after me, but where else am I going to go?*

Before I had a chance to call or message Bear, Sian replied: *Fuck off, cuz,* she wrote, *I'm in Chiang Mai too! I arrived this morning and, last night, I felt really down. Like I needed someone from home – and now you're here. Come and meet me ASAP.*

Talk about a sign from the universe. I called Sian, and we decided to travel around Thailand together for the next few weeks. Then I relayed this plan in a message to Bear, adding, *I'll be in Phuket in a couple of weeks' time if you're still around?* He wasn't impressed, but told me to 'stay in touch'.

A lot happened over the next few weeks. Sian and I travelled to multiple beautiful islands – an experience I will treasure in my heart forever. Eventually, we ended up in Phuket, alongside Theo, Bear, and Bear's best friend, Alan. After a very boozy reunion, Bear and I slipped back to our old ways – we were all over each other.

After a few too many drinks on a crazy night out in Phuket, we booked a trip to visit magical Phi Phi Don Island. Bear and I staggered back to our hotel room, giggling about our impending boat trip, which was due to leave in six hours' time. 'How the fuck are we going to get our shit together for an 8 a.m. departure?' I said, bumping like a skittle into Bear, against the corridor walls.

Somehow, we managed to catch the ferry but, bloody

hell, it was a choppy seventy-minute ride. We were all massively hungover; Theo spent the entire journey throwing up over the side of the boat. Bear and I carried on drinking – and flirting.

When we arrived on Phi Phi Don, Bear insisted we should share a hotel room. 'Your cousin can get her own room,' he said, snaking his arm around my waist.

Sian decided not to join us on the first night out but didn't explain why. By the time I woke up, she'd gone. *Sorry, G, but I just don't like Bear's energy,* she said in a text message. *I'm heading back to our hotel in Phuket. I didn't want to ruin your time or make you feel as though you need to leave. I'll see you once you head back. Have fun and call me if you need me.*

I felt bad that I hadn't noticed Bear was making her feel uncomfortable, but I knew I would see her in a day or two and, at this point, I had no reason to think that I wasn't safe with Bear. He'd been so sweet to me so far.

Okay, babe, I replied. *Text me when you're back.* Then the day descended into chaos, the night into misery.

The carnage started that afternoon on Monkey Beach. While paddling along the sugary shoreline, a monkey bit my calf. I wheeled around just in time to see its needly teeth pierce my skin, sending an agonising stabbing pain up my entire leg. I screamed my head off. The monkey let out a maniacal screech too. Blood gushed from my wound, colouring the sea. I screamed but nobody came to my rescue. It was like a scene from *Jaws*; everyone, Bear included, darted in different directions – away from the primate and me. When the monkey eventually released my leg, it cackled and lolloped along the beach away from me.

I'll give Bear his due, he came to the hospital with me. He also lent me money for the bill – because I'd lost my credit card. Fortunately, I didn't need stitches, just a top-up rabies shot and a course of antibiotics. 'You'd best not come near me tonight,' laughed Bear in the taxi back to the hotel, 'I don't wanna catch rabies.'

Back at the hotel, Bear and I went up to our room. Everything seemed cool between us; we had a laugh about my monkey episode and Bear was over me like a rash as we showered and dressed to go out. His demeanour soon changed when a group of teenage girls checked into the next room.

We got chatting to the four girls, backpackers from Australia, over drinks on our respective balconies. Bear started giving it all the banter. 'We're going out later – probably heading down to the beach for a party. You girls should come ...'

I estimated the average age of those girls to be around eighteen or nineteen. They were lovely, so I also urged them to come out with us. Being the only girl in our group, I was excited for some female company. 'Hopefully see you later, girls,' I said before they headed back into their room in their flip-flops, giggling. Then I turned to Bear, who was suddenly solemn behind his shades. We were due to meet Theo and the others for dinner. 'C'mon, we should get going. I'm starving.'

'Yeah, I'm not feeling great – got a bit of a dodgy stomach coming on,' said Bear, draining his glass.

Stupidly, I turned all Florence Nightingale, didn't I? 'Oh, don't worry babe, we don't need to go out. We can stay in, watch a film or something. I can nip to the pharmacy, get something for your stomach. Shall I get you a—'

'No, it's okay. I'll be fine.'

'Well, shall I look after the room key, then?' I offered. 'Just in case.'

'No, I'll take it – I told you, I'm fine. Just relax.'

Fast-forward a few hours, and Bear's stomach ache had eased. He did come out with us, but he was grumpy as fuck over dinner, then happy as Larry when we bumped into the Australian girls at the beach bar. What Bear did next disgusted me to the core.

We were all sitting in a circle on the beach, drinking and laughing. I was trying to chat to a couple of the girls but I had one eye on Bear, who was blatantly making a move on their friend, snaking his hand around her naked waist, nibbling her ear. He didn't even look at me. Instead, he started snogging the girl – right in my face.

I was too embarrassed to say anything. *How could he do this to me?* In public, too. I dropped my face into my hands, and when I looked up, Bear was on his feet, hand in hand with the girl, still kissing her as they vanished into a crowd of partygoers brandishing glow sticks.

Knowing Theo would stick by my side, I decided not to let Bear's antics spoil my night. *If he'd rather be with a teenager than me ... more fool him.* I even continued partying with the girl's friends – at the end of the day, they hadn't done anything bad to me.

I stayed on the beach with the others for a while, but soon I began to panic. All I wanted was to grab my stuff and get as far away from Bear as possible. My leg was throbbing from the monkey bite and I needed my antibiotics, which were in the room – along with my phone charger and the rest of my stuff.

When the beach bar closed, we went back to our hotel for more drinks, but by now, I desperately wanted to get my belongings. So, I headed up to the room and knocked on the door. Silence. He'd locked me out. I knew Bear was in there, having sex with the girl he'd kissed on the beach.

She told me as much when we introduced ourselves in the lobby two hours later. Her name was Angela, and she was sitting alone beside a stand loaded with bright flyers advertising excursions when I hobbled in around 4 a.m. – after spending two hours trying to sleep on a sunbed by the pool. Angela's neck, shoulders and arms were patterned with love bites. 'Did Stephen Bear do that to you?' I said, eyeing the reddish-blue marks.

Angela looked mortified. 'Oh, shit, is he your boyfriend?'

I lifted my shoulders. 'Nah, not really.' I wasn't angry at Angela – she wasn't to know. I felt more concerned for her than anything; she looked so young.

'Oh, I'm so sorry. I wouldn't have gone back with him. I wouldn't have done all those things with him if I knew you two were together.'

'He's not my boyfriend. We've been sharing a room and sleeping with each other for the last few days. Look, I'm a girls' girl. Worse shit happens – I got bitten by a fucking monkey on the beach yesterday.'

We both laughed – because sometimes you've just got to laugh when things turn to shit, haven't you?

I ended up sleeping in Theo and Alan's room – then Bear woke us up, frantically knocking on the door at 9 a.m. Theo opened the door and Bear hurried in, rambling on. 'Babe, babe, it ain't what you think. It ain't how it looks.'

By now, I'm thinking, *He's got a split-personality disorder.*

'For fuck's sake, Bear, just let me get my stuff and get back to my cousin. I literally hate you now.' God, trying to get out of that hotel was a nightmare. Bear let me back in the room, then followed me around as I gathered my stuff. 'You've got it all wrong, Georgia. Honestly, babe. Please, hear me out.' Theo had to hold him back so I could escape.

Bear's dramatics didn't end there.

My phone didn't stop pinging during the ferry journey. That was Bear, flooding my inbox with more deluded rants. At the same time, I was messaging Sian and Mum, telling them what had been happening. Sian said, 'Just get back as soon as you can.' Mum was calling Bear all the names under the sun. Theo texted me: 'Please can we use your hotel shower before we catch our flight home? Bear's not with us.' So, I typed the address of the hotel I was trying to get to and sent it to Theo – that was the least I could do after he'd let me sleep in his room. Ping, ping, ping – Bear again: 'You've got it all wrong.' 'I haven't slept with another woman.' 'Please believe me, Georgia.'

I was gobsmacked. Everyone saw him with Angela. *Does he really think I'd buy this utter bullshit, even for a second?* Even if he hadn't slept with another girl – which he had – he'd abandoned me on a night out in Thailand – and locked me out of our room, knowing my credit card was blocked and that I needed my medication. *Just fucking leave me alone. You made it clear you didn't want me last night, so why are you chasing me now? This is all such a head-fuck.*

Bear must've followed Theo and Alan. How else would he have known where to find me? I hadn't told him the name of the hotel where Sian and I were staying. I'd not long arrived back there myself when I came face-to-face with him. He bombed into the reception, soaking wet, wearing nothing but shorts, trainers and a deranged smile.

'Georgia, you've got it all wrong. Just give me one minute to explain.'

My head was about to explode from listening to his repetitive bullshit. 'Look, you're imagining it,' he went on. 'I didn't sleep with another woman. Please, you're the only girl for me. Let me—'

I lost it then. Bear was trying to gaslight me, and I'd had enough. Raging, I grabbed a couple of paperbacks from the bookshelf beside me and lobbed them at him.

'You lying, disrespectful prick,' I screamed, throwing more books.

Bear ducked this way and that, trying to beat a path through the missiles and, just then, the manager came running up to me, flailing her arms. 'Why are you throwing books? Stop throwing books.'

I paused, clutching a hefty thriller. Bear stopped in his tracks too, grinning. 'I'm sorry,' I said, 'but, you see that scumbag over there ... He locked me out of our hotel room to have sex with another woman, and now he won't leave me alone – even though I've made it clear I want him to go.'

The woman gasped and pointed at the bookshelf. 'Throw books, throw books,' she said.

I chucked the thriller at Bear, clipping his shoulder as he ran past me, through the back door and out to the pool area. Snatching another book, I chased him in my platform sandals, yelling, 'You wanker!'

A guy by the pool filmed our fight on his phone, capturing me running after Bear, book in my hand, out the back gate and into the street. 'Jesus,' he moaned. I hurled my last book at his back when he fled.

My reaction bruised Bear's ego. As the footage hit the internet, he trash-talked me with vile Instagram posts in which he tried to make me feel insignificant compared to his previous girlfriends.

Just don't call me your ex, he wrote, responding to my post seconds earlier about my serial cheating 'ex'. *You just got rumped and dumped*.

The press jumped on the story, many outlets headlining with Bear's foul comment. Reading those articles, I felt hurt, humiliated and inadequate. I vowed there and then: *I never want to see or speak to Stephen Bear again.*

You're probably asking yourself how and why I first fell for Bear's lies – and continued to do so. Despite everything, I maintain we should always see the best in people. I used to think Bear would recognise the good in me and, in return, treat me with decency. But I now know he has zero empathy. His brain just isn't wired that way. I ran headfirst into his traps, believing he wouldn't disrespect me. Unfortunately, he did.

Relationships are invariably challenging. I don't think I'm alone when I say this. Nowadays, I focus on the positive qualities I'm looking for. I want a man who is patient and loving, for example. I want a man who's consistent, who shows up for me. I don't think this is too much to ask for, is it?

'BE HONEST AND
SPEAK YOUR
TRUTH. THE
UNIVERSE FAVOURS
AUTHENTICITY.'

'JUST BE PATIENT,
BEAUTIFUL SOUL,
AND TRUST THE
UNIVERSE. THE TRUTH
ALWAYS COMES
OUT EVENTUALLY.'

Chapter Three

TAKING BACK
MY TRUTH

SUNDAY 2 AUGUST 2020, DEBDEN, ESSEX

I read his message a few times, debating – in my hungover state – whether to respond.

From memory, the text said something like: *Why don't you come over for a cup of tea? I'm feeling shit, you're feeling shit . . . What's the worst that can happen?*

First, I thought, *Why is Stephen Bear inviting me over for a cuppa first thing on a Sunday morning? I haven't seen him in almost a year.* Then snippets from the night before flickered through my mind.

I'd been at a party with Theo, who'd messaged Bear to say the three of us should meet (Bear was at another party nearby). Anyway, I didn't hook up with Bear – it got late, we were pissed, you know how it is – but scrolling through my phone, I noticed I'd also exchanged a couple of messages with him in the early hours.

I sat up in bed, cringing at my texts, in which I'd admitted feeling low and isolated following the Covid-19 lockdown. This was true; like much of the population I'd struggled mentally amid all the social restrictions and 'bubble' rules. But why the hell was I telling Bear all of this? After our explosive row in Thailand the previous summer, I'd vowed never to speak to him again.

As I dragged myself out of bed, another message landed on my phone. Bear again, saying he'd stick the kettle on and get the biscuits out, or something similar. I'll admit, I laughed to myself. *Since when did Bear do Sunday morning tea?* I hit reply: *Yeah, okay, I'll be over in an hour or so.* After all, it was only a cup of tea. And as he'd pointed out, *What's the worst that could happen?*

I don't need to justify my reasons for going to Bear's house, but in case you're wondering, I thought our meeting might help clear the air between us. Despite our history, I hadn't forgotten the fun times we'd shared. Bear was somebody I enjoyed being in the moment with; although he'd humiliated me, at no point had I fallen madly in love with him (although he probably imagines that I did). He hadn't won my heart as Jake had done. My relationship with Bear had always been more of a friendship and lust affair. *Maybe we can be mates again*, I thought.

So, on that sunny Sunday morning, I poured myself a strong coffee, swallowed two paracetamols to calm the techno dancers in my head, then got ready to see Bear. As

I was only nipping over the road for a cuppa, so I didn't bother with make-up or fuss over what to wear. I just scraped my hair extensions into a high ponytail, slung on some Nike gym gear – black leggings and a crop top – stepped into my trainers and headed out the door.

I'd anticipated an awkward atmosphere, but as soon as I hugged Bear hello, I sensed a mutual let's-be-friends-and-put-our-shit-behind-us vibe, which suited me.

Bear was being his usual cheeky self. 'So, have you missed me, then?' he asked, plonking a mug of tea before me on the breakfast bar.

'Yeah, Bear,' I said, 'But I'm only here to be friends – nothing more than that.' I was being strong while also enjoying his company again. He sat down opposite me, sipping his tea, and within a few minutes we were laughing and taking the piss out of one another. I think I cracked a joke about how the lockdown must've impacted Bear's love life, which he took with good humour. He told me he'd missed me, but neither of us mentioned our bust-up in Thailand or the twisted message he'd posted about me on Instagram afterwards: *You just got rumped and dumped.* Our Sunday morning cup of tea was all about rebuilding bridges, seemingly.

Maybe I should have gone home after that. Would things be different now if I'd said, 'Look, this has been lovely. Thanks for the tea. See you around?' But I'll never be able to answer this because that scenario didn't happen. Bear made me feel good about myself, which was just the lift I needed back then. So, when Bear suggested getting out for a bit, I thought it was a good idea. *What's the worst that can happen?*

Bear bulleted off his stool, grabbing our empty mugs as he did so. 'We ain't gotta do anything big or nuffink,' he said. 'I need to get my car cleaned – just come with me. It's no big deal.'

'Yeah, cool. I've got nothing planned today, anyway . . . too hungover.'

Off we went in Bear's Merc, windows down, radio blaring. He was acting a bit manic now: jittery, talkative and laughing to himself. I gave him a look that implied, *You're nuts*, and let him get on with it. I found this comical, cartoonish side to his personality endearing.

As planned, Bear got his car washed. Then he said, 'Right, we're going to Melin now. Dunno about you but I'm starving.'

I gestured at my leggings. Melin, an extremely popular Turkish restaurant in Woodford, has a strict dress code. I couldn't rock up there in my gym gear and trainers. 'I can't go to Melin like this, Bear. They won't let me in. I'm not going there.'

'Shut up, you look sexy,' said Bear with a wide grin. 'Anyway, it's cool. They all know me in there. They ain't gonna turn "The Stephen Bear" and his beautiful friend away. C'mon, it'll be a laugh.'

I felt like a right scruff when we sat down in Melin ten minutes later. The manager couldn't have been more accommodating though, turning a blind eye to my outfit and greeting Bear as though he were royalty. 'Stephen, how've you been, my friend? Welcome back to Melin,' he said, shaking Bear's hand. 'Where would you like to sit?'

I'd promised myself I wouldn't drink alcohol that day but, before I knew it, Bear and I were knocking back tequila shots. We weren't alone; scanning the other tables I noticed that most people were getting stuck into the booze, letting their hair down after months cooped up at home, no doubt.

As the drinks flowed, I no longer cared about being in my gym gear; I was having too much fun. My body melted with the mellow live saxophone music. I can't recall exactly what Bear and I talked about over lunch – it was just silly banter, really – but I remember we didn't stop laughing. Bear recorded a few little videos for his Instagram Stories, but I warned him: 'Don't put any pictures of me up. I don't want people knowing we're together right now.' Bear was cool with this, his attention quickly diverted when the waiter reappeared with our two final tequila shots.

What started out as a civilised cup of tea in Bear's kitchen had morphed into a drinking session. Any previous doubts I'd had about seeing Bear were drowned by alcohol. The more I drank, the more I fancied him again. I could literally feel my dignity slipping away with the day. One voice in my head groaned, *You're going to make a mistake here*, while another sang, *Life is for living. You're single. Go with the flow, enjoy the moment.* The latter voice won me over when Bear suggested going back to his place. 'It's still early. We could sit in my garden for a bit, have a drink. Nothing big . . . What d'ya reckon?'

'Give me a second.' I picked up my phone, which I'd left

screen-down on the table throughout lunch. There were no missed calls, no messages, nothing about Bear and me on socials, and the clock confirmed the day was indeed still young – just past 2 p.m. I necked the tequila, soured my mouth with lime, then smiled, saying, 'Yeah, why not?'

Bear's garden, boxy and secluded by high fences, trees and bushes, made the perfect environment for enjoying a quiet drink, I figured. If we'd gone to a bar, we'd have risked being videoed or photographed by some random punter quick to contact the press. Although I was drunk, I knew the tabloids would lap up footage of Bear and me out together, especially as I'd publicly promised never to see him again after his 'rumped and dumped' attack. So, yeah, I felt safe in Bear's garden, relaxing in a comfy arm-chair on his stage-like decking, guzzling a glass of chilled Chardonnay, away from prying eyes. *Perfect*, I told myself.

We sat together at Bear's garden table, drinking wine and laughing as we reminisced about our early days together on *The Challenge* in Namibia. Less than a minute into our conversation, Bear shot up. 'Fancy another drink and a game of Fives?' he said, already making for the kitchen door.

'Yeah, go on then,' I said. Bear's mention of 'Fives' alone made me all nostalgic inside. The card game was our 'thing' in *The Challenge* villa.

I knew then, as Bear clanked around in the kitchen, that we wouldn't sit there for the rest of the day pulling our best poker faces over games of Fives. And I won't lie, I was up for some no-strings fun. *I shouldn't feel ashamed*, I told myself. *I've slept with Bear multiple times before. He's treated me badly in the past, but we're both consenting adults – and I don't want a relationship with him. It'll just be sex.*

Bear returned, dropped a deck of cards on the table and uncorked another bottle. He mucked about with the cards for a bit, excited to show off his 'tricks', which, to be honest, I was too drunk to follow. Our game of Fives didn't get off the ground either. We couldn't keep our hands off each other, let alone focus on jacks, kings or queens.

My cards fluttered to the ground as we kissed. Bear held my face and stroked my hair, whispering, 'God, you feel good,' between breathy kisses. I surrendered to his touch, inhaled his familiar citrusy scent: Sauvage, by Dior. Then he was like, 'Give me a blow job,' and without going into too much detail, I obliged – at that moment, I was more than up for it.

During that, I somehow managed to wriggle out of my gym wear before Bear planted both hands around my waist and lifted me with him as he stood.

I'll spare you the graphic details of what happened next – because the acts I consented to were supposed to remain private – but in a snapshot, Bear and I had sex for twenty minutes that day (longer than he'd ever lasted before). Directing those proceedings, Bear was very specific about which sexual positions we should perform at certain locations. He carried me to various points around the garden, suggesting a new position at every stop. Our session finally ended with more sex in the kitchen.

Afterwards, we had a couple more drinks in the garden.

I was knackered and drunk but sobered up quickly when Bear casually announced, 'Oh, by the way, babe, I think some of what we just did might have accidentally been caught on my CCTV cameras.'

'What do you mean, you *think?*' I was confused more than anything. I hadn't spotted any cameras in the garden. 'I mean, Bear, mate, you know if you've been having sex in front of a camera. Are you telling me I've just been filmed having—'

'Oh, chill out, chill out, it's no big deal. I wouldn't do it on purpose – and it might not have recorded. Anyway, I . . . '

By now my eyes were ping-ponging, scanning the garden for cameras. Bear's words sounded like they were coming from deep under water. I felt sick and disorientated, wondering whether he was just being cheeky, having a laugh. His grin said he might have been joking, but I needed to find out.

I pushed my wine glass across the table. 'Look,' I said calmly, 'If there's footage of us having sex then I need to know about it, otherwise I'm gonna wake up in a panic tomorrow.'

'All right, chill out. C'mon, I'll show you the recording now if you like?'

Bear showed me the footage on a television screen in his kitchen. The first section showed views of his garden and kitchen in night-vision mode. 'Ah, I'll forward it to daytime,' said Bear, like we'd just settled down to watch bloody *EastEnders.*

He fast-forwarded the video, pressed play, and there I

was with Bear, naked and animated inside eight separate rectangles. The cameras had captured most of the sex positions Bear had instigated. I gaped at the television. 'Fucking hell, Bear, how long does this go on for?' Seriously, the video was never-ending. 'How ... what the ... you've got to get rid of this,' I said. 'I didn't know you had cameras. I didn't know I was being filmed. Why didn't you tell me about the cameras? Why ...?' I had so many questions but the bigger deal I made the more Bear tried to gaslight me.

He went on a rant, 'Look, it ain't a big deal. I'll AirDrop the footage to your phone just now. You ain't gotta worry what's on there.' He picked up his phone and transferred the video to mine. 'There, that's all I've got. You can watch it tomorrow. I didn't know the cameras were filming, y'know.'

I pointed at the television. 'But it's still on *there*.'

Bear grabbed the back of his neck with both hands and looked at the ceiling. 'Yeah, but I'll delete it ... end of. You're blowing this out of proportion, George. You've had a nice day – we've had some fun ... Why have you got to be like this now?'

I calmed down slightly then. Maybe Bear hadn't known the cameras were filming after all? Plus, he'd mentioned – and shown me – the footage, which he was now promising to delete. 'Well, we *must* delete it,' I said. 'I'll die if anyone else sees it.'

Bear reassured me several times that evening that he wouldn't show the video to anybody else. Later in bed, however, he sent the footage to a friend on WhatsApp – as

I lay right there beside him. I snatched the phone out of his hand and burst into tears. 'What the fuck have you just done?' I said, blinking at the still image of Bear and me in the missionary position and the two ticks below it that had not yet turned blue. I threw the phone onto Bear's chest. 'Unsend that now – and fucking delete it.'

'Okay, don't worry, it's cool. I only sent it to a family member – they're not gonna do anything with it. Look, I've unsent it.' He pushed the phone towards my face, so I could see he'd retracted the video message.

'A family member? Why the fuck would you send a video of me and you having sex to a relative? What's wrong with you? Look, this is serious. If this gets out, I'll get you done for revenge porn.' I was bolt upright now. Bear remained slouched against his silver velvet headboard.

'Do you think I'm fucking stupid? I wouldn't send it to anyone. You can go to prison for that.'

'But you *did* send it to someone.'

'I unsent it, what's the problem?'

'I promise you, Bear. I'll go straight to the police. I never gave you permission to film that video. You didn't tell me ...' I broke down again, tears of shame, humiliation, regret and fear streaming down my face.

'Oh, don't cry, babe,' said Bear, his voice softening. He put his phone aside and spread his arms. 'Look, come here. I promise you, George ... you can trust me. I've deleted the footage. It's gone. I didn't mean to upset you. I'm sorry – I really am.'

I fell into to Bear's arms, and cried into his

tattoos, believing he would remain true to his word. How wrong I was.

Despite Bear's insistence that he'd erased the video, I still felt panicky the next day. As soon as I got home, I WhatsApped him, saying, *Promise me you won't do anything with that video?* Again, he said he'd deleted the footage, but questions plagued my mind. *Had he made another copy behind my back? Did the footage still exist on his CCTV hard drive?* I told Mum and a couple of close friends about the film, and they reassured me. 'Look, we all know what Bear's like when it comes to girls, but I'm sure you've got nothing to worry about,' said Mum. 'What happened is private between you and Bear – he won't want a sex tape of himself getting out. He'll be thinking of his *own* career and reputation, don't forget.'

Mum had a good point. Even when Bear and I weren't speaking, I knew I could turn to him for friendship and support if I needed to. We'd always had each other's backs professionally too. Bear and I both had reality-TV projects in the pipeline around that time; the industry was beginning to pick up after lockdown. *Yeah, he has enough respect for me – and himself – not to ruin our careers*, I told myself. *Stop agonising over this, Georgia. Move on.*

A month or so passed without incident, my friendship with Bear still intact. During that time, Mum and I even went to the launch of his sunbed salon, Bronzing Bear, in Buckhurst Hill, Essex – and posed for press photographs alongside the life-sized bronze bear sculpture he'd installed outside the shop. There was no animosity or awkwardness between us at the opening. 'I'm really proud of you,' I told him – because I *was* proud of him. I could see his business doing really well. He already had the entire cast of *TOWIE* queuing up to top up their tans. I came away from the launch feeling quietly confident that the whole sex-video saga was behind us.

One Saturday evening, about six weeks after Bear 'deleted' his home video of us having intercourse all over his garden, I went out for a meal with some girlfriends. I was having a lovely time until my mate's boyfriend, Liam, rocked up.

While chatting away with the girls about the Maldives – I was taking Mum there on a work trip later that week – Liam appeared at my shoulder.

'For fuck's sake, Liam, you scared the shit out of me,' I said. He literally did make me jump – he looked as white as a sheet. I didn't know Liam that well – and his girlfriend, Sarah, wasn't even out with us that night.

Liam said he needed to talk to me about 'something'.

'Go on then,' I said.

'Erm, it's probably best I tell you this in private.' Liam mined his hands deep into his jean pockets, cocking his head towards the door.

I laughed, thinking, *This is weird*. 'Nah, it's okay, this lot know everything about me already.'

'Ah, right, okay then, but if anyone asks, you didn't hear this from me, right?' He inched towards the table, shoulders hunched. 'So, my mate's just told me that Stephen

Bear showed him a video of you giving him – Stephen – a blow job. Obviously, I know you wouldn't do something like that, Georgia, but please don't say I said anything – cos I don't want these boys knowing I told you.'

I didn't notice Liam leave the restaurant. I went into proper shock, had a little cry about it to my friends. 'What shall I do, girls?' I sobbed. 'Do I go to the police?' Then, somehow, I managed to force the matter to the back of my mind for the rest of the evening. *I'll deal with this in the morning*, I thought. I was too emotional to make serious decisions.

But the new dawn brought little hope in my efforts to get to the bottom of Liam's story. When I spoke to Sarah, she said Liam didn't want to give an account to the police. 'Liam doesn't want to get involved, Georgia,' she said, 'he just felt he should tell you what he'd heard. It's probably bullshit, anyway. You know what boys are like.'

What could I do? The police wouldn't investigate my claims without solid evidence. And if I did go big with this, it'd become public knowledge in no time. There was no point reaching out to Bear; I'd already made it clear, multiple times, that he shouldn't show the footage to *anyone*. If he hadn't listened to me then, he wasn't going to listen now – especially as I had no proof of him sharing our video, which I now believed he had done.

In the end, I reached out to Bear's brother and told him about the CCTV recording. I knew that Bear highly respected his sibling, a well-respected businessman and family man. *Maybe Bear will listen to his brother if he intervenes,* I thought. *Hopefully he'll foresee the monumental damage this situation could do to our families.*

'I don't know what to do,' I said, 'this is out of my control. Bear filmed us having sex without my knowing – and now he's showing that video to people. I *know* he is. Please can you speak to him? This is my final warning . . . I can't have this video getting out. This is my last attempt to deal with this before I go to the police.'

Bear's brother said he was appalled that Bear hadn't warned me about his CCTV system but doubted his brother had shared the footage. 'I don't think he'd do that,' he said. 'He's had lots of famous girlfriends in the past – some for long periods of time. Maybe he took sex pictures or videos with them? If so, he's had plenty of opportunities to share those images. Why would he do this now . . . to you?'

I agreed with him. Bear's exes were far more famous than me. He did speak to his brother for me though, which I massively appreciated. Bear told him he hadn't shown the video to anyone – because he'd deleted it and, again, I felt reassured. Even if he was lying, surely he'd listen to his brother and stop this madness. I went to the Maldives with Mum, truly believing, this time, that the video had gone away for good.

In late November 2020, Britain went into lockdown again. Still in the Maldives with Mum, I had two choices: fly home with Mum and isolate in my flat, or go to Dubai, where I could spend the next six months working as an influencer.

I chose the latter option – even though I, and other influencers, got a lot of stick for it in the press. At that time, international travel was banned under UK lockdown rules – apart from limited exceptions such as work. I didn't break those rules as I flew direct from the Maldives to Dubai. And besides, my mental health and finances were crumbling – I couldn't face being locked-up alone in my flat.

My first week in Dubai was amazing. I worked hard, creating tonnes of content for my followers on social media – and partied hard with the reality-TV crowd who'd also escaped to Dubai for the season. My *Love Island* mates Ellie Brown and Kaz Crossley were there, among other girls I knew, so I was never short of somebody to go for a daytime cocktail with. Bear was also in Dubai, posting Instagram Stories capturing his wild nights out. I did my best to avoid him. Seemingly, I couldn't. I'd been in Dubai less than two weeks when my worst nightmare unfolded.

I was having a drink with Ellie at Cove Beach Club when I received a private Instagram message from a man in America who ran *The Challenge* Tea Page – a website where fans share all the latest show gossip. The message subject line was *Have you seen this?* I gagged when I opened the image: a screenshot, showing Bear on top of me in his garden. Hands slick with sweat, I messaged the man back: *Oh my God, where did you get this? I need to know right now – because that's me in this picture.*

He replied instantly: *I think it's on Stephen Bear's OnlyFans page. I'll try to find a link for you.* I'd heard rumours that Bear had recently joined OnlyFans, but I didn't know anything about him being a sex worker. Turns out he was incredibly active on OnlyFans, where he'd apparently posted – among other explicit videos of himself with various girls – a clip from the CCTV footage that he'd filmed without my consent. Footage that he was selling to his thousand-plus subscribers on the adult-only website.

I fell into Ellie's arms, sobbing as I tried to explain my horrific news. 'It's Bear ... he's ... put ... a video of us having sex on OnlyFans. How could he be so fucking stupid? How could he be so heartless? How many others have seen it?'

Ellie hugged me. 'Surely there's a way to remove it from the internet,' she said. I don't think she knew what else to say in this fucked-up situation.

I exchanged a few more messages with *The Challenge* fan-page guy before he deactivated his Instagram account. I couldn't even access the footage – because internet restrictions in Dubai blocked graphic sites.

Back home, Mum was bombarded with messages as news of my exploits with Bear spread like wildfire. She called while I was still in contact with *The Challenge* fan. I sobbed into the phone, 'What am I gonna do, Mum? I'm so ashamed. I shouldn't have done it. It's all my fault – I shouldn't have slept with him. How do I make it go away?'

Mum was devastated too, but kept it together for me, as always. 'Listen, sweetie,' she said, 'you haven't done anything wrong. We'll fight this. We'll go to the police. But first we'll need to prove that he [Bear] posted this video himself.'

Wrought with shame, I wanted to disappear, but Mum was right. Traumatising though it'd be, I *had* to see the OnlyFans content – and find out how it got out there in the first place.

So, I posted this message to my Instagram followers: *If anyone has seen or heard of this video including me in Bear's garden, please send it to my agent (I added Mum's email address as she was my agent then). Thank you x.* Then, for context, I wrote: *If an ex was to film me on a hidden camera in an environment where I felt safe and then sent it to people ... that's gotta be a heavy stretch pending, surely?* I signed off with a bear emoji.

At this point, I didn't know the sex video had gone viral, appearing on the world's biggest online porn platforms, leaked to millions. I'd hoped a few people would message Mum, but a flurry of emails flew into her inbox – all showing screenshots of the video on various platforms. The video had attracted millions of views, prompting Bear to up the price of his OnlyFans subscription to £50.

Internet trolls littered my social pages. *I like that video of you being fucked all over the garden. It's cool,* wrote one sicko. *Congrats hon, you're a porn star now,* said another.

As more screenshots of the video appeared in my Instagram inbox, Bear sent me a furious WhatsApp voice note. 'George, man, what the fuck are you going on about? My DMs are flooded,' he raged. 'Everyone's going on, saying I filmed you and sent it, so then I've gone on to your story, and you've actually written some fucking essays, painting me as something I'm not.'

My flesh crawled. He was trying to manipulate me, hoping I'd feel sorry for him.

'I've done nothing wrong. I don't do stuff like that – that's next-level shit. It's really not fair,' he continued.

I typed my response, explaining that people had sent me screenshots of the video. *I'm getting you nicked*, I warned.

'You've actually lost the plot,' said Bear in his next voice note. 'Fucking hell, do your worst and you're gonna feel so fucking dumb afterwards.'

Wicked, I wrote back, *we'll discuss it in court. Cause you know what you've done.*

Meanwhile, Mum received an email containing a link to an OnlyFans video emblazoned with Bear's tag. She'd also been sent an advert for the video, dated 8 November 2020. The ad, sent from Bear's verified OnlyFans account, 'Steviebear @hollywoodbear', and peppered with purple devil emojis, read: *Morning everyone can't wait for you to see me fuckin in my garden … here's a little sneak peak. I'll be droppin this video tonightttt.*

It was now 9 December. 'He must've have been selling this video for over a month,' said Mum.

A part of me died when I saw the screenshot beneath that vulgar advert. The image showed me, on my back in Bear's garden, with him naked and on top of me. I thought Bear at least had some love and respect for me as a human being. No. Bear's true feelings for me were out there for the whole fucking world to see. He'd literally sold me. In one fleeting post, he'd sold my innocence, my dignity, my body and soul. He'd stolen my confidence and joy. Bear regarded me as nothing but a price tag: his object to sell.

Within days, 'Georgia Harrison sex tape' became a top search on Google. Fortunately, an OnlyFans employee deleted Bear's video and deactivated his account, but the footage was still elsewhere online.

From Dubai, I spoke with Michelle Roycroft, an ex-police officer and family friend, who advised me to report the matter. I gave a full account to Essex Police, knowing that revenge porn is notoriously difficult to prove. A third of all cases are dropped by the victim. Revenge porn is legally described as 'The disclosure of a private sexual image without consent – with intent to cause that person distress'. So, you need to prove that the perpetrator intentionally distributed the material.

I couldn't face going home – everybody was talking about my video and the UK was still in lockdown anyway. Too ashamed to go out, I shut myself away in my hotel room. Every day I'd cry for hours, blaming myself for having sex with Bear. *It's my fault. I should never have gone to his house that day.*

In the interim, Bear showed zero remorse, posting videos of himself out partying in Dubai, spending the cash he'd made exploiting me while bemoaning the closure of his OnlyFans account. He insisted the woman he secretly filmed in his garden wasn't me. 'It's complete lies,' he said in one of his pathetic videos. 'It's clearly not her. As I said, the last time I saw her was in Thailand.' This was yet another slap in the face. *Hadn't he done enough damage already?*

*

I hid in my hotel room for several days before I tried social-
ising again, at a boat party. Big mistake. Naturally, friends
wanted to speak to me about the Bear situation – to show
their support – but I didn't want to bring them down. I
sat alone, drinking and crying as the party whirled around
me. I felt trapped. How I longed to see a familiar face
from home.

Talk about a serendipitous moment: just as the boat
pulled into the dock, Jake messaged me. *Georgia, I heard
about the Bear thing.*

My heart sank for a moment as I wondered, *Oh God,
what does he think of me?* I hadn't spoken to Jake for a few
months. *I'm in a really bad place*, I replied. *So, it's good to
hear from you right now. I'm stuck in Dubai.*

Jake called me then. 'Luckily I'm in Dubai too,' he said. I
can't tell you how wonderful it felt to hear his voice. 'Text
me your address and I'll come over.' I staggered back to my
hotel, feeling blessed and excited, but still shocked that
Jake was here in Dubai.

I'll never forget Jake's first words when he stepped into
my hotel room, 'God, Georgia, you look like you've just
seen a ghost.'

'I feel like I have,' I said, and we came together in the
tightest, safest hug. 'Thank you for coming,' I cried into
his chest.

'I'm always here for you. You know that, don't you.'

I nodded, unaware that it would be one of the last times
I'd see Jake alive.

*

As Christmas neared, the stress of the Bear sex video scandal took a massive toll on me. Still stranded in Dubai, I grieved for my former self while trying to stay resilient. The online haters continued to hurl abuse at me. *Serves you right for having sex*, was a common comment. Brands I'd shared great working relationships with before stopped hiring me as an influencer. That said, a handful of sex toy companies wanted me to promote their latest dildos. Of course, I said no.

I wasn't looking after myself. My diet suffered; I'd sink a bottle of wine every night just to numb my emotional pain. My face erupted with acne. I looked like shit. Then, two days before Christmas, I began to feel unwell, like proper shivering and stuff. Assuming I'd caught Covid, I decided to isolate in my room – nothing new there, eh? – until the symptoms passed. I kept thinking, *What's your luck, Georgia?* Later that evening, my symptoms got worse. I woke up in bed trembling, pyjamas glued to my skin. I called Mum who said, 'You've got to see a doctor immediately, Georgia. Promise me you'll go?'

It's a good job I took Mum's advice. I nearly didn't, though. Being in Dubai, I couldn't just nip along to a local GP surgery; it's a taxi-to-the-hospital job over there – and I was worried that might cost an arm and a leg. Plus, I didn't want to infect anyone if I did have Covid. In the end I had no choice – I felt so horrendous. In the taxi I turned into a delirious iceberg. I barely recall arriving at the hospital. The next thing I knew, I was hooked up to a drip, a doctor looming over me, grave-faced as he said, 'You're very lucky,

Miss Harrison. If you'd left it another twenty-four hours, you might not have made it.' Apparently, my body had gone into septic shock – brought on by a burst ovarian cyst. My pelvis had become infected, and my organs were beginning to fail, the doctor said. I could've died.

I spent Christmas in hospital in Dubai, but this didn't bother me. I was just thankful to be alive, to be honest. My friends – Kaz Crossley, Danny, Nicole and her partner Tom – visited me on Christmas Day, armed with presents. Gradually, my fighting spirit returned. Instead of lamenting what could've happened, I chose to put a positive spin on my health scare. *I'll get home, get sober and fit, and fight fucking tooth and nail for justice. Not just for me, but for all other victims of revenge porn.* I finally left Dubai on 27 December. I went to Los Angeles – because I still wasn't ready to face the music back home – or living opposite Bear.

Bear was arrested at London Heathrow Airport when he returned from Dubai on 15 January 2021 – his thirty-first birthday. He was released on bail, pending charges.

At times, I worried the charges against Bear would suddenly be dropped. He looked to be having the time of his life in his TikTok videos. Then, four months later, DC Brian Sitch, investigating officer at Essex Police called me. 'Good news,' he said, 'the Crown Prosecution Service [CPS] has authorised charges against Stephen Bear. So, he's going to be charged with two counts of disclosing private sexual images – which is the revenge porn part, and voyeurism, for recording a sexual act – and the fact he recorded it in his garden.'

The best possible outcome would be for Bear to plead guilty. But deep down, I knew he wouldn't hold his hands up to this. I'd already agreed to waive my anonymity. Now all that remained, presuming Bear denied the charges, was for me to stand up in court and tell the truth – just as I had all along.

'IN EVERYBODY'S
LIFE THERE WILL
COME A TIME WHEN
THE ONLY CHOICE
YOU HAVE IS TO BE
STRONG. EMBRACE
THE BEAUTIFUL
POWER OF RESILIENCE
AND RIDE THE WAVE
OF UNCERTAINTY.
IT'S ALL PART OF
YOUR JOURNEY.'

'BE GRATEFUL
THROUGH THE
BEAUTIFUL MOMENTS
AND RESILIENT
THROUGH THE TOUGH
ONES. WE CAN'T
CHOOSE EVERYTHING
LIFE THROWS AT US,
BUT WE CAN CHOOSE
HOW TO HANDLE IT.'

Chapter Four

TAKING BACK
MY CONSENT

**TUESDAY 6 DECEMBER 2022,
9.A.M., LOUGHTON, ESSEX**

W/*hat if he walks into the courtroom in a lovely shiny
suit, acts like a decent human being and paints me as
a psychopath? He's a master manipulator who can cheat his
way through anything, using his underlying charisma to win
people over. I should know; he's done this to me so many times.*

Argh, the worries rattled in my head as I stood in Mum's
kitchen, manically ironing my white shirt. I was imagining
how Stephen Bear might look and behave at the opening
of his revenge porn trial.

As predicted, Bear had pleaded not guilty to all three
charges against him relating to explicit CCTV footage of
us having sex in his garden in August 2020. Today he'd

appear in court, accused of filming that footage without my knowledge and selling it on porn websites, making at least £2,181 in the process.

There was no doubt in my mind that Bear deliberately posted our sex video online – and I'd gathered the evidence to prove as much. My life had been hellish since the video went viral – the impact had all but ruined me emotionally, professionally and financially. But to win justice, I'd now need to prove, in a packed courtroom, that Bear intended to cause me distress by publishing our intimate exploits for the whole fucking world to see.

Mum and I knew Bear and his legal team would try to discredit me. Anxious thoughts continued racing through my mind, They'll say I'm promiscuous because I chose to have sex with him in his garden. Bear will make up all kinds of crap about me – then those lies will be all over the media. What if the jury believes him over me?

I felt like I was the one who was about to stand trial. My nerves were jangling. No joke, I'd already necked at least ten coffees since I'd woken up. But, hey, at least my shirt was immaculately pressed. Now all I needed to do was change into the suit I'd had specially made, do my hair and make-up, and get to Chelmsford Crown Court.

Looking respectable in court was important to Mum and me. Not only was it courteous to dress smartly for a judge, but we obviously wanted to be taken seriously. And if Bear's recent social-media posts were anything to go by, he had also given his court outfit fair consideration.

Two days ago, Bear had launched a poll on Twitter,

asking his followers to decide which colour suit he should wear to his trial. I didn't give a shit about his fans' suggestions. The fact he posted this vote in the first place spoke volumes about his mindset concerning the serious charges he faced. To him, this was all a laugh at my expense. I could just imagine him saying, 'I'm gonna get let off for this bullshit. I'll get done up in a smart suit, look like a respectable, upstanding citizen, give 'em the Stephen Bear charm, then get on with my life.' I'd already heard him say words to this effect.

He'll probably pull the wool over the jury's eyes with his dramatics, I thought – then Mum came into the kitchen, phone in hand and a bemused look on her face.

'Oh my God, Georgia, you must see this. Look at the state of him.' One of Mum's mates who was already at Chelmsford Crown Court – we were lucky to have full support from all our close friends and family – had messaged pictures of Bear's arrival there. My heart did a merry dance when Mum brought up the images on her phone. I replied, 'Fucking hell, he looks like a glorified pimp.'

Honestly, we both had to laugh at those photos. There he was, stepping out of a white Rolls Royce, dressed in a flamingo-pink suit and tie. A massive black fur coat was draped over his shoulders and he was clutching a cane topped with a gold snake's head. He had sunglasses on – even though there was snow on the ground – and was smoking a fat cigar. Oh yeah, Stephen Bear had come as his authentic self: top to toe, through and through. Bear's latest girlfriend was with him, matching his look with sunglasses and a pink top teamed with skin-tight black leather trousers, holding his hand and pouting for the cameras. Mum said, 'I must say, Georgia, I think Bear's done you a massive favour.'

I agreed; seeing those hideous pictures gave me a much-needed confidence boost as I put on my suit and headed to court with Mum, ready to stand up to the narcissist who'd stripped me of my dignity. I'd waited a long time for this moment – and it hadn't been easy.

Bear's trial was originally set for 7 February 2022, but it was postponed at the last minute. Mum got a call from the Witness Protection Service (WPS) two days before the original trial was due to begin, saying proceedings had been moved to December because Bear's defence team needed 'more time' to prepare his case. I sobbed my heart out when I heard this; over a year had already passed since Bear's arrest. In that time, I'd lost a lot. I had to rent my flat out and move back to Mum's – mainly for financial reasons but also because I couldn't face living opposite Bear any longer. Then my best friend, Cenk, passed away. I was still grieving and, more than anything, I wanted the trial over and done with. I'd lost a year of my life while Bear had gained a year to get his shit together. Now I faced a further nine months of torture.

Suddenly, I was back where I first started: struggling with my mental health; struggling with my finances; struggling with my shame; struggling with my grief; struggling with fucking everything – while Bear uploaded X-rated videos he'd made with his girlfriend on porn sites and social media. He even captioned one of the video posts with *At least she knows I'm filming her.*

Bear was incorrigible online. On the day when his initial trial got postponed, he posted a video on TikTok in which he and his girlfriend cavorted in matching orange death-row prisoner jumpsuits. From then on, he flooded the internet with pornographic home videos. My friends and followers forwarded the material to me. There was one film of him humping his girlfriend beside the mirrored wardrobes in his bedroom, her shouting, 'Fuck me, Daddy,' throughout. A montage he posted on Twitter featured more of Bear and his girlfriend's sexual exploits on a beach in Italy. I mean, each to their own, but I believe Bear's chief motive for posting these videos was to try to antagonise me. He even shot a video in his garden; in this footage his girlfriend gives him a blow job.

Amid his outpouring of mucky films, Bear also went live with his girlfriend on social media to protest his innocence ahead of the trial. I saw this broadcast in which he branded his charges 'fake news'. 'This whole saga is going to come to an end and I can get my life back to normal,' he said. 'I can get back on TV and work with big brands like before. There is no evidence against me because I didn't do what I was accused of doing. I reckon it'll be thrown out. I'm the nicest person in the universe.' Bear was arrested and admitted breaching his bail conditions after that outburst. Meanwhile, as he consistently pulled stunts to goad and hurt me, I couldn't publicly defend myself as doing so would jeopardise the trial. Now, after twenty-one months of being silenced, I was about to tell my side of the story. In a courtroom, in front of Bear and his friends and relatives. In front of my friends and relatives, lawyers, the judge and jury. I was bloody petrified.

As I expected, the media circus was in full swing when Mum and I pulled up outside the court. Before we got out of the taxi, Mum squeezed my hand. 'You can do this, Georgia,' she said. 'You've got nothing to feel ashamed about. We're all behind you. What you're about to do is incredibly brave – I'm so proud of you. I love you, sweetie.'

I felt so blessed. Bella; my stepmum, Leigh; Dad; Michelle Roycroft; my Aunty Sharon; and Mum's best friend, Michelle Sugar, had arrived at court, too – here to support me.

I gave Mum a kiss, managed a nervous laugh. 'Oh, Mum, don't – I'll be in floods of tears before I even get to the witness stand at this rate.' I knew Mum was nervous too, even though she hid it well. 'Thank you,' I said. 'I couldn't have come this far without you – you've been amazing.' I said a silent thank you to the universe too – for giving me the strength to be here today, and I swear I heard Cenk's voice, clear as a bell in my head: *Go in there and give them everything you've fucking got, Gee. I'm right there beside you. I'll guide you through this.*

'C'mon, then,' said Mum, 'let's do this.'

Mum and I were taken to separate witness rooms inside the court. We weren't allowed to see each other again until after we'd both given our evidence, so that we couldn't discuss our evidence or the trial, which we couldn't watch until we'd both finished in the witness box.

I was called in after Mum on the first afternoon of the trial. When a woman from the WPS had showed me around the courtroom a few days earlier, I'd refused the option of giving my evidence from behind a screen. 'No, I don't need a screen,' I'd insisted. 'Because I'm not lying – I have nothing to hide.' But I'd since changed my mind; on reflection the witness stand was too close to the dock and, to be honest, I didn't want to give Bear the fucking benefit of looking at me again.

Walking into the courtroom, I was so glad I'd opted for the screen. I don't think I could've got through the ensuing hours with Bear's eyes on me. He'd be scoffing and sneering at my every word, no doubt. All morning I'd psyched myself up for this, but as I sat down behind the screen and scanned the jury – nine men and three women – my heart walloped like mad. Reciting my oath, I didn't recognise my voice. I wondered how much detail the jury had heard so far. *How had they reacted to the prosecution's opening speech?*

Thankfully, the prosecution barrister, Jacqueline Carey KC, put me at ease. She was gentle in her approach, first asking me why I'd chosen to waive my anonymity. I looked at the jury, then at the booklet on the table in front of me – *That'll contain stills from the CCTV footage*, I realised – and lifted my chin. 'I've chosen to waive my anonymity because it disappeared the moment the footage surfaced. Stephen Bear hung me naked on a wall for millions of people to see,' I said. 'And I don't want any other woman to go through this.'

Jacqueline nodded and then instructed the jury and me to open the booklet. This was the part I'd been dreading: twelve people whom I didn't know from Adam, seeing pictures of me naked and engaging in all manner of sexual positions with Bear. Images taken from footage I thought nobody else would ever see.

Lifting the cover to that dossier, I felt so vulnerable, but I knew I had to just go with it. Part of Bear's defence was that the woman in the garden footage, dated 2 August 2020, wasn't me. I wished it wasn't me, too – but it was. Looking at the first photograph, which clearly showed a side view of me, legs in the air with Bear on top of me, filled me with heavy regret and shame. *Why did you do this?*

'If you could please turn your attention to page four of the document,' said Jacqueline. *Oh, God*, this image showed me performing a sex act on Bear. My stomach turned all maggoty as Jacqueline then asked the jury and me to turn another page, then another, and so on. 'Miss Harrison, can you confirm that's you in the image?' Jacqueline asked with every page turn.

'Yes, that's me,' I said firmly, over and over, adding, 'I consented to sex with Stephen Bear – but I didn't know I was being filmed,' once I'd viewed the final picture showing Bear and me doing it bloody doggy-style on his kitchen floor. I think the jurors were as embarrassed as me. They made no eye contact with me throughout the viewing of those photographs.

During a brief pause in proceedings, I had a flashback to that day in Bear's garden. I remembered the sex – it was far more dramatic than it had been before with Bear. The stills from the footage spanned his entire garden, the photographs proving Bear hadn't once strayed away from the cameras. He'd been passionate and romantic throughout, too – kissing me, stroking my hair and carrying me from one spot to the next as he directed me through multiple positions. At no point did I think, *There's no emotion involved here.* Now, I felt so utterly ashamed, like I'd really let myself and my family down. How did I allow such an awful person, who clearly didn't give a fuck about me or my mental health, manipulate me in this way? Although I knew deep down that I wasn't to blame, I was still kicking myself, thinking, *I'm a fucking idiot – I gave Bear all the ammunition to violate me.*

Jacqueline continued with her questions. She asked me to relay the sequence of events from 2 August 2020, so I told the court that Bear and I had both been hungover that day. 'We went out for lunch, then went back to his house for drinks,' I said. 'I was feeling drunk when we went outside to his garden to play cards.'

I explained how Bear and I had then had sex in his garden, reiterating that the event had been 'a lot more exciting, a lot more dramatic than usual, when I look back'.

'He [Bear] told me afterwards that his CCTV cameras in his garden "might have captured us having sex". He showed me the footage – and I told him, "If anyone sees that, it's going to change my life, it's going to change yours".

He told me I was being "really uptight", and "exaggerating something that wasn't intentional".'

Next, I told the jury how I'd seen Bear send the video to 'a family member' on WhatsApp – and how I'd then made him unsend it. 'He promised to delete the video and said he wouldn't send it to anybody else,' I said. 'I was crying because I then realised that potentially he was going to spread it – and I realised the situation I'd got myself into. I was upset because I'd thought he had respect for me.

'I told him it would completely ruin my life and ruin his career, and if he wants to send it to anyone it would be revenge porn, you go to prison for revenge porn, and I would call the police.'

When Jacqueline asked when I first became aware that the footage had been posted online, I recalled the moment I received the screenshot from *The Challenge* Tea Page guy, which he'd seen on Bear's OnlyFans page. I said, 'I have never given Stephen Bear permission to upload or show or distribute that video to anyone. It's definitely me [in the video] but for a while he was trying to say it was someone else. I was really emotional and infuriated. I was adamant that I would be seeking the help of the criminal justice system. I couldn't do it by myself.'

I was in the witness box for the entire afternoon. That evening, I had to stay in a hotel to prevent me from discussing the trial with anyone. I barely slept, unable to rest as I recalled everything I'd said in court. I wondered what the jury had made of my account – *Do they think I'm a slag?* Graphic frames from the garden footage played a menacing slide show in my head. *Will Bear get away with this?* I also felt huge sadness at the person Bear had become. *How could the man I once trusted have done this to me?*

The next day, I returned to my seat behind the screen, this time to be cross-examined by Bear's defence barrister, Gemma Rose. I'd been dreading this part of the trial as, undoubtedly, Bear's lawyer would do everything in her power to try to get him off on all charges. I was also fully aware of how difficult it is to get a conviction for revenge porn – and of how I needed to prove that Bear intended to cause me distress.

This was the moment in the trial when I wanted to appear at my strongest, but I broke down soon after Gemma questioned how I could prove that it was Bear that had uploaded the video to OnlyFans.

'Did you see, with your own eyes, Stephen Bear upload the footage?' she asked.

I wiped away my tears as I remembered a second advert that'd appeared on Bear's OnlyFans page. An advert I *knew* that he'd posted – just as I knew he'd deliberately uploaded the footage. In that advert, Bear had urged people to: 'Sign up now for 50 per cent off to see me fucking this bitch in my garden.'

'I knew it [the footage] originated from him but I did not think he would be monetising it on a verified account. That is so stupid on his part and so evil,' I said. My voice juddered. I pictured Bear, sitting in the dock in his pimp suit, flashing his girlfriend looks across the courtroom that screamed, *I'm getting away with this.*

I took a couple of deep breaths and continued, 'It [the video] was on his [Bear's] account for a month. *That* is the evidence. I have seen screenshots. I have seen the promotion when he puts me at "50 per cent off".'

Gemma waited a few seconds, then she said, 'You used the term "revenge porn". Are you only saying that now because of these charges?'

My inner strength fought back then – and I meant every word that came out of my mouth. Nothing but the truth. 'I am using those words because I am 100 per cent confident that's what it is,' I said. 'I wanted to make clear to Stephen Bear what would happen if he sent those videos.

'It upset me. It ruined my life. I thought he had respect for me. There was a time when he said he respected me, he loved me, and at the time I thought he had a promising career on television, and he would not do what he did. But looking back, I was an absolute idiot.'

I verified that I'd consented to having sex with Bear. 'But I didn't for a second have any idea there was CCTV in his kitchen or garden where we were having sexual intercourse,' I said. 'He [Bear] was leading. I was drunk and obviously not thinking it would come to anything like this. I didn't think he would do this to me. We had a lot of history, and he knew the effect this would have on my life.'

My evidence seemed to go on forever, but I stuck to my guns, enforcing that, yes, I did agree to have sex with Bear but, no, I didn't know I'd been filmed – and, yes, he *did* distribute the video for financial gain.

The trial went on for a week, during which I was a

nervous wreck. The prosecution called more witnesses to the stand, including police officers who'd arrested and questioned Bear at London Heathrow Airport and Matthew Redden, the online enforcement analyst who'd kindly not charged me when he'd removed the sex video from PornHub and various other websites. He told the court how Bear had increased his OnlyFans subscription prices from $20 to $50, adding that the footage had also appeared on the online forums Telegram and LPSG.

I didn't sit in on Bear's evidence – because I couldn't bring myself to look at him. Every day during the trial, he put on a theatrical performance for the press, turning up at the courthouse in his rented Rolls Royce, carrying that ridiculous snake's-head cane and puffing cigars. He was papped kissing his girlfriend in an alleyway close to the court. Bear was loving all the attention – and this sickened me.

Of course, I subsequently read the press coverage of what Bear had to say about me and the video. The court heard he was £12,000 into his overdraft around three weeks before he set up his OnlyFans account. Up until the account's deactivation, he'd earned just under £40,000. He'd made around £2,000 of that sum from the garden video.

Bear, while disrespecting the barristers and judge – and everyone else in the courtroom – by swearing through his evidence, spun a web of lies. When asked how I reacted to the footage, he said, 'You would think it's funny, you know what I mean? She laughed. We played it on the monitor screen. We watched it back on that and then she asked for a copy of it. Straight away of course, I said, "I will send you a copy". Straight away she told me to delete the footage. Straight away, no questions asked [I deleted it]. Why would I want that on my phone? My intention was to catch up with a friend – sex was a bonus. To be filmed is quite funny.'

Bear bragged about sleeping with other famous women he'd met on OnlyFans. Jacqueline asked him if he was using his evidence to tell everyone how many people he'd slept with. 'You'd better move on as you're starting to look a bit silly,' was Bear's arrogant response before moaning, 'I nearly lost my house because of this, that's what no one else sees. I've got all day.'

Another lie to spill from Bear's mouth in court was that I apparently told him he looked like a 'fit Paul Daniels' when he'd performed card tricks at the garden table before we had sex. I'd never even heard of Paul Daniels – I had to google him – so how could I possibly have made that comment?

When the jury retired to consider its verdict, just before 4 p.m. on 12 December, I couldn't imagine what the outcome would be. My head was spinning with it all as I tried to weigh up the prosecution and defence's closing arguments. Jacqueline had told the jury not to convict Bear on the basis that he 'sleeps with people and doesn't call them back'. Regarding other women he had unnecessarily mentioned during the trial, she added: 'He [Bear] broadcast their private sexual lives in an open court and gave no thought to their privacy at all.

'He gave no thought about whether they wanted to

have it broadcast in that way, in a public arena. And that's because he doesn't care about it.

'It gives him fame, it gets him notoriety. He will say whatever he wants, he will do whatever he wants, he will distribute whatever he wants.'

Gemma, on the other hand, said Bear had accidentally filmed the footage. 'This isn't a court of morals,' she'd warned. 'You may not even like Mr Bear, you may not agree with the way he handled himself at the time . . . but that isn't a reason to convict him of this case.' She'd also pointed out that Bear's OnlyFans account wasn't set up when the video was filmed. 'You don't have [information] from OnlyFans [about] who sent the video, who uploaded the video; in these circumstances can you really be sure?' Gemma ended her argument by saying Bear 'simply didn't know' whether our video had appeared on OnlyFans, which I knew was bullshit. He knew exactly what he was doing. But the question was, who would the jury believe? The prosecution or defence? Bear or me? Still, I worried that the jury would deem me a slag who should've known better. *Or maybe the jurors will be sympathetic? Maybe some of the jurors have daughters of their own? If so, how would they feel if they were exploited like me?*

I would have to wait another day to find out.

The jury returned just after 3 p.m. on 13 December. Initially, I refused to go into the courtroom. 'I can't bear to see his reaction if he gets off,' I told Mum. 'And I don't want him to see me – I won't be behind a screen this time.'

In the end, Mum convinced me to go in to hear the verdict. She seemed confident the jury would convict Bear on at least one or two of the charges. 'I'm pretty sure this is going to go in your favour, Georgia,' she said. 'If you don't go in, you're letting him win – and he's gotten away with too much already.'

So, I went into the public gallery, conscious not to give Bear as much as a fleeting look. At that moment, I felt so grateful for the emotional support from my family and friends. We stood in a line, Mum holding my right hand, Dad holding my left. My stepmum, Leigh, was there, as well as Michelle Roycroft, the ex-police officer who'd advised me and had become like a third mum to me (Michelle is a real hero), my half-sister Darcey, and Star, Bella and Rachel.

I was literally shaking all over when the foreman of the jury rose. A rush of heat shot to my head as Judge Christopher Morgan addressed him, 'Have you reached a verdict for all of the charges?' he asked.

'Yes,' said the foreman. I squeezed my eyes shut. *This is it. Fuck, this is really happening now.* The judge asked how the jury found Bear on the first charge of revenge porn. Silence, filled with whisperings behind me.

'Guilty.' Mum and Dad's hands tightened around mine. My heart thrummed in my ears. Then came a second, firm, 'Guilty,' followed by a third, and I wanted to punch the air or scream, 'Yes,' or something, but I didn't. I kept my mouth shut, responding instead with dignified silence ... and tears. My friends and family cried, their love and relief for me shining brightly. Seeing them so emotional reminded me just how much this case had affected them too.

After the verdict, Bear suddenly piped up, saying, 'In my opinion, from the very beginning it was never a fair trial. What the press said against me ... I was fighting a losing battle and it is what it is.'

It took all my will not to respond to this ridiculous statement. Bear's actions – his ridiculous costumes and social-media posts, kissing his girlfriend in front of the paps – had made this the most talked-about case in the British media. He wanted that attention – he *created* it, so to insinuate that he got an unfair trial was downright ludicrous.

The judge cast Bear a weary look. 'Thank you for that observation,' he said before bailing Bear and setting a sentencing date for the following month.

I got a glimpse of Bear as the security guards led him away. He looked pissed off, shuffling in his Louboutin shoes. We've done it. *After all this time and stress, I've won justice. Now, I can speak.* I felt inside my suit pocket for the folded piece of paper holding the speech I'd prepared as Mum kissed my face. 'We did it,' she said through her tears.

'DO WHAT'S RIGHT
FOR YOU. IGNORE
THE OPINIONS OF
OTHERS. YOU ONLY
GET ONE LIFE – LIVE
IT YOUR WAY.'

'FOLLOW YOUR INTUITION AND SPEAK ONLY WORDS OF TRUTH. THE WORLD VALUES INTEGRITY.'

Chapter Five

TAKING BACK
MY VOICE

MONDAY 13 DECEMBER, 2022,
CHELMSFORD CROWN COURT

All the shame and guilt I'd carried for the last twenty-eight months evaporated with those three clear verdicts of 'guilty'. Stephen Bear had been convicted of revenge porn and voyeurism. The jury had believed my side of the story, validating my belief that I had been right to fight my case in court.

The verdict couldn't erase the damage done – I would never forget how Bear had violated me by secretly filming us having sex and then broadcasting it to the world. Reliving my trauma in the witness box – collectively studying the explicit imagery from that fateful day in Bear's garden with the jury – had drained every ounce of strength from my body and mind. But as I walked out of the court-room, I felt empowered. Like I'd regained my dignity. I wasn't the first – and inevitably won't be the last – victim of image-based sexual abuse. Now I wanted to do everything in my power to help others affected by this horrible crime. By going public about my ordeal, I hoped to inspire fellow victims to also fight for justice. To make my voice heard, loud and clear to the world, that committing such despicable acts is totally unacceptable. I started my crusade there and then, outside Chelmsford Crown Court.

I'd spent the entire week working on my victim-impact statement, praying I'd get to read this version rather than the one I'd prepared for a 'not guilty' verdict. By now, the internet was saturated with headlines shouting: *Stephen Bear convicted of sharing sex tape* and *Stephen Bear found guilty of sharing sex tape of ex-girlfriend Georgia Harrison in 'revenge porn' trial* and so on, accompanied by more photographs of Bear and his girlfriend arriving at court that morning, when he'd made a peace sign with his fingers for the cameras. I must say, however, that the press treated me with utmost respect throughout the trial. The paps hadn't monstered me; they'd just quietly snapped away from a distance whenever they saw me outside the court. Today, I felt grateful to be standing before the massive media crowd thronging the courthouse steps, with television cameras and booms and microphones in my face. I welcomed the explosions of flashes and the chitter-chatter of camera shutters.

Mum stood beside me as I recounted what I'd endured at the hands of Bear:

The only way to describe how I am feeling now is relieved. The last two years have been absolute hell and this verdict will allow me to start to put the pain I have suffered in the past and start embracing the future.

Bear's behaviour was completely unacceptable and those who choose to commit such crimes should and will be prosecuted. We are living in a time where so much of our lives and our children's lives are spent online and it is so important that individuals are protected in the virtual world, just as they are in reality. Social media has given us the egalitarian belief that we are all publishers, but what it hasn't done is regulate what we should responsibly publish.

I hope me taking a stand gives other men and women who have fallen victim to revenge porn the courage to seek justice and, most importantly, show them that they have absolutely nothing to be ashamed of. I have felt ashamed, hurt, violated, even broken at times, but today I stand here feeling empowered, grateful and a huge sense of unity with all of those who have reached out to support me throughout this ordeal.

I want to take the time to thank the Essex police force, especially Brian Sitch, and also Michelle Roycroft, who have been such a huge support to me throughout and have worked tirelessly for two years to get to this point. I also want to thank my KC, Ms Carey; the jury; the judge, Christopher Morgan;

and all of the victim support team at Chelmsford for ensuring justice was served and helping make my experience as comfortable as possible. And, of course, my friends and family for being by my side. Especially my mum, who I couldn't have done this without.

Thank you.

I went for a meal and a few much-needed drinks with my family after delivering my statement. Today I could finally celebrate my twenty-eighth birthday, too – albeit a day late. It felt good to relax, to raise a glass and speak openly about my case without worrying about prejudicing the trial or feeling ashamed. Celebratory messages flurried on my phone. People praised me for being 'human' and 'honest', which meant the world to me. My speech had obviously resonated with the British public.

Naturally, the predominant question raised over dinner that evening was, 'What will happen to Bear?' He was due to be sentenced on 31 January 2023, which seemed a long way off to me. The maximum punishment Bear faced was a two-year prison sentence. Other options included community service or a suspended jail term. Anyway, Bear would only go down for the maximum stretch if Judge Christopher Morgan deemed his offences to fall within category one for harm and culpability. For this to happen, the judge would rule that Bear's acts caused me 'very serious distress' with 'significant psychological harm'. Bear could also end up on the Sex Offender Register, according to my legal team. Mum reckoned Bear would definitely go to jail. 'We know how difficult it is to get a conviction for revenge porn – yet the jury found him guilty on all three charges,' she said. 'The jury saw how distressing this has been for you, Georgia – that was bloody obvious. He's turned your life upside down. He's got to go down for this.'

I wanted nothing more than for the next six weeks to whizz by but, typically, time dragged. Although I could now speak publicly about my court case, I was yet to get full closure – and I needed this as I worked on getting my life and career back on track.

Aside from all the beautiful messages I'd received from fans on social media, there remained some nasty people who saw fit to slate me. Those who thought I'd deserved to be exposed in such a heinous way online – just because I'd decided to have sex one day like any other normal human being. Others thought that my non-consensual appearance in a sex tape that Bear posted to millions meant I'd want to view their sexual antics. One geezer sent me a video of himself having sex with his wife as they both shouted my name. I mean, what the fuck? Fortunately, I managed to rise above those reactions. Such people weren't worth my energy.

On the afternoon of 30 January 2023, the day before Bear was due to be sentenced, Jane, my contact at the Witness Protection Service, called me. 'I'm sorry,' she said, 'but Stephen Bear's sentencing hearing won't be going ahead tomorrow. It's been postponed until the third of March.'

Oh my God, I was raging. 'Postponed? Why? Bear was

convicted in the middle of December.' I couldn't get my head around it. Adding to my fury, the woman explained that Bear had appeared at a court hearing earlier that day.

'The judge has asked for a psychiatric report to be conducted on Bear, hence the delay I'm afraid.'

'Psychiatric report, on Bear?' *I could knock one up in fifteen minutes.* This was a huge blow. Yet another delay. Meanwhile, Bear appeared to be living his best life. A few weeks ago, he'd filmed himself proposing to his girlfriend at the Moulin Rouge in Paris. He posted the video on TikTok with a caption declaring: *She said yes.* He further commented on the post: *That was best moment of my life so far. Not only did over 5,000 people see that in the Moulin Rouge in Paris. But it broadcasted live on the streets of France next to the Eiffel Tower for 100s of thousands to see.*

Jane apologised again – although it wasn't her fault. I read about Bear's 'mention hearing' on the Essex Live news site later that day. During the hearing, Bear's lawyer, Gemma Rose, said a probation report had suggested the psychiatric assessment on Bear because 'those who have assessed him so far were unable to formally diagnose'. A full psychiatric report would be 'beneficial' to the court, she said. Judge Christopher Morgan warned a warrant for Bear's arrest could be issued if he failed to show up on 3 March 'without good reason'.

The delay did set me back, but around this time I was lucky to chart my journey in a documentary for ITV titled *Revenge Porn: Georgia vs Bear*, which would be broadcast after Bear's sentencing.

Following the trial, several production companies had reached out to me, keen to document my full story. I chose to go with MultiStory Media, a subsidiary of ITV Studios, because the network had been good to me – it gave me my first break in *TOWIE* – and, as you already know, one of my top manifestations was to 'get my own ITV show'. (However, I never expected that my dream ITV show would involve my telling the nation how I was exploited in a sex video.) Also, I trusted the crew, who shared my vision for the documentary: to come across as an everyday girl who'd had something serious happen to her. I wanted to be my authentic self and tell the truth after being silenced for so long while Bear posted on his YouTube channel, doing his best to discredit me with his lies.

The documentary team was amazing, giving me full sign-off on which footage would be used. My video diaries, which I'd started when I first found out Bear had sold our film online, would also feature in the documentary. In these clips I show my vulnerable side. You see me sobbing after Bear's trial was delayed, when I feared I would never get justice. I wanted viewers to see every emotion I experienced throughout the sex-tape affair – to know what was happening inside my head. I was thrilled to be working with the award-winning producer/director Candace Davies, of whom I'm a huge fan. I particularly loved the 2019 documentary she made with Little Mix's Jesy Nelson, *Jesy Nelson: My Story*, which painted such an insightful and sensitive picture about body shaming and mental health in the age of social media. Candace became my trusted friend and companion, someone who not only held the camera but also held up my spirits during moments when we weren't filming. I trusted Candace wholeheartedly with my story – I couldn't have told it without her.

On Friday 3 March 2023, the ITV camera crew accompanied Mum and me to Chelmsford Crown Court for Bear's sentencing hearing. I wasn't cutting my best look today though. Yesterday, Jane had called to say that the hearing might be deferred again due to a 'complication'. Then she'd phoned me back early that morning. 'You'll be pleased to know Stephen Bear's sentencing hearing will go ahead today after all,' she said. But I'd already worked myself into quite a state. I hadn't stopped crying since her previous call. Unable to sleep, I'd stayed up until 4 a.m., alone and sobbing while watching episodes of *Game of Thrones*. I was scared that Bear might not show up at court and we'd face yet another delay. Now I had huge, frog-like eyes and I'd broken out in spots all over my face. *Oh well, this is what I wanted to be: the real me*, I thought.

I didn't see Bear arrive at court as I kept my distance again, but I heard he'd posed for selfies with his fiancée outside the court before breaking into a chorus of Chris de Burgh's song 'The Lady in Red', his rendition aimed at a female reporter in a scarlet coat. Bear also moaned to onlookers about 'not getting a fair trial'. 'You're innocent until proven guilty,' he shouted.

'But you were found guilty,' reporters replied in unison. Bear's behaviour didn't surprise me in the slightest. I was just glad he'd showed up as I couldn't face another delay. I wanted this whole saga to be over, to get my documentary out there and feel normal again.

At least Bear wasn't in his pimp outfit this time, opting instead for a dark grey suit. I sat in the public gallery with Mum – Bella and Rachel were there too – clenching and unclenching my stomach muscles. *Will Bear go to prison? I really hope so.*

For all the delays we'd encountered in the case so far, proceedings on the sentencing day happened relatively fast. First, I read my victim-impact statement to the court. I managed to speak calmly, and, surprisingly, without crying, while not casting Bear one look.

> I'm making this statement to tell the court the impact this awful crime has had on me. I've always been a very open and trusting individual who is happy-go-lucky and sees the best in everyone.
>
> During my time in the spotlight in regard to the media, I have always been extremely cautious when it comes to taking any sort of explicit photos or videos. It has always been my worst nightmare that a photo or video of me that was meant to be kept private would surface publicly, so therefore I haven't ever captured any sort of seriously explicit material even on my own device. When Stephen filmed me without telling me, it not only stole that choice from me, but it also seriously affected the way I trust people.

When I first saw the screenshot of the footage and realised it had actually been sold online by him, I just felt physically sick. I was crying hysterically for hours and having panic attacks on and off. I suffered from anxiety on a level that many will never be able to understand. The scale of how widespread the video had gone was just unimaginable. Everywhere I went in public, people were talking about it: many to show support, but still it was hard to have to discuss it. Even when people were talking about different subjects, I just couldn't physically be present in the room, my head was just whirling with thoughts of what was going on and the fear that more of the footage could resurface any second. As if the pain of having to know all my friends, ex-partners, family and colleagues, past and present, were aware of it wasn't bad enough.

To make matters worse, I also had to deal with him [Bear] ridiculing me on his social-media channels to millions of people. The accusations ranged from [claiming] it wasn't me in the video, to I was aware of the footage, to he hadn't seen me in two years. It was such a lot to deal with and he spent a lot of time mimicking me and doing impressions of me crying which just made me feel even worse.

The trolling got completely out of hand and still continues to this day [to] do so! Millions of people were on my profile and 'Georgia Harrison sex tape' was one of the most searched things on Google when you type in my name. Even now when I have to do a live video with a company on any of my channels, every single comment is about the video or about Bear and it is so hard to ignore – plus it's embarrassing for whoever is running the brand page, as instead of discussing their product, every comment is just a nasty troll comment that I have to try to ignore.

There was a time when I really did love Bear, both on a relationship level and as a friend. To think that he intentionally filmed and sold footage of me, knowing full well how much it was going to affect me, has really left me feeling very hurt, embarrassed, insignificant and insecure in many ways. I do not have the same confidence I used to have when it comes to going for new jobs or the potential of a new relationship. I always have this situation in the back of my mind, and just think, 'They're not going to want me when they find out.' I feel so ashamed of myself for sleeping with him in that situation, and it makes me feel sick to think so many people have watched it. It just makes me feel humiliated, disgraced and, quite frankly, mortified.

I spent so long crying and having to deal with all of the stress and anxiety that my physical body pretty much deteriorated in the weeks following the incident. I have videos of me on my birthday, just crying my eyes out, covered in boils and spots which came up within days of the incident. I started to become physically ill about a week later and was rushed to hospital where they said I had multiple infections in my organs, including my bladder, kidneys and ovaries. I had a cyst [that] burst, too, and the doctor said if I had stayed home one more night, I could well have died from sepsis, but I literally didn't want to leave my room – my mum had to force me to. I ended up spending five days in hospital on my own, which happened to be on Christmas Eve, so I spent the whole of Christmas alone in hospital during which time he continued to ridicule me online and sign up to other sex platforms to continue with his 'work'. Which he is still doing now.

I still occasionally suffer from panic attacks, and I will never want return to my own home in Essex because I can't stand to be near him. He is so impulsive and I'm so afraid as I just don't know what he is going to do next.

I have reached the point where I just want all of this to be over so I can get some justice, some closure and put this whole situation as far behind me as possible. It is also my hope that this case changes the way some platforms handle this sort of situation.

The courtroom was silent as I stepped down from the stand. A profound sense of relief that I'd made it through my speech flooded through me.

Next, there was some legal discussion about the psychiatric report on Bear. My barrister, Jacqueline Carey KC, recommended a custodial sentence on the basis that I'd suffered 'emotionally and financially'.

The only section of the hearing that went on for too long, I thought, was when Gemma Rose started talking. Seriously, I could have made and cooked a shepherd's pie in the time it took her to rattle off excuses for Bear. Bear has 'delusions of grandeur and distorted thinking', she concluded at the end of her mitigation speech. 'He accepts the verdict but still maintains his innocence. He is willing to work in the community,' she added. Mum shot me a worried look as the judge ordered Bear to rise. A football team played in my stomach; my hands were coated with sweat. *God, please don't let him off with community service.*

'A custodial term is the only appropriate punishment,' the judge began. He said Bear had lied to me when he claimed he'd deleted the garden footage. He praised me for speaking out, saying I'd endured 'extensive humiliation and embarrassment'. Then he sentenced Bear to twenty-one months in prison, placed him on the Sex Offender Register, and slapped a restraining order on him to not contact me for five years.

I heard a few people in the gallery say, 'Yes!', but Mum and I remained silent. I glanced at Bear before he left the dock to start his jail term. He didn't look at me, but he gave the court a little wave on his way down to the cells. 'Have a good evening. Enjoy your weekends, everyone,' he said. I knew then that prison was the best punishment for Bear. I just hoped he'd see the error of his ways and come out of jail a better person.

Outside the court, I stood on the steps again to speak

to the press. I kept my statement short but to the point, stressing that I had no regrets about waiving my anonymity.

'Today's sentence is a vindication of what I've been put through, and it sends a clear message that the police and the courts take this matter very seriously.

'I want to let all other victims of this crime know that I stand in solidarity with them. I hope that this puts anyone off committing this sort of crime and for anyone who has been a victim of it, I hope it gives them some sort of justice. Thank you so much for all your support. And that's it.'

A cameraman shouted, 'Well done', and the entire press pack cheered and gave me a round of applause. I clapped with them. It seemed rude not to.

One thing I knew for certain following Bear's imprisonment was that I really wanted to help other victims of revenge porn – or 'image-based sexual abuse', as it is more appropriately known (many victims feel 'revenge' insinuates that the victim has done something wrong).

As my story went huge in the press, I received tonnes of DMs from women who had been through similar traumas. I've got to say, the reaction to my case has been overwhelming; I've had women coming up to me in the street, often crying as they tell me their personal stories. Sadly, many of the victims who've contacted me have been unable to secure convictions for the perpetrators of the crimes against them, mainly because their cases got dropped due to a 'lack of evidence'. In other cases, the courts had decided 'intent to cause distress' had not been proved. This riled me; you shouldn't have to prove intent. Anybody who sends sexual images or videos of someone else without their consent should know full well the pain, distress and hurt it's going to cause them.

While filming my documentary, I interviewed Ellesha. She told me how an ex-partner had been arrested after explicit videos of her appeared on PornHub. My interview with Ellesha is available on YouTube and she has kindly given me permission to share her story in this book.

Like me, Ellesha says she was sent a link to footage on PornHub. She told me, 'The person who sent the link said, "I don't want to worry you, but ..." So, I was quite concerned at that point. And the minute I opened them [the videos], and realised what they were ... and that they were of me, I was absolutely devastated.

'Once I'd gone on to the PornHub page, there were hundreds of likes on there. There were comments on there. It also showed how many people had downloaded it, put it on to other websites and who had sent it to their friends. You've just got no scope of understanding how far this has gone.'

Ellesha reported the footage to the police, but the CPS later decided there wasn't enough evidence to charge her alleged perpetrator. 'That was devastating, really devastating,' she said. 'You try to carry on, but you always have that residual anger that you've had to go through that whole process. It's humiliating. It's a really embarrassing process. I had to tell the police everything, then for it to end the way it did was just the worst.'

I could really see the pain in Ellesha's eyes when she spoke to me. Her experience reminded me so much of mine. The emotions she'd described – anger, embarrassment, the sheer devastation when you realise somebody has shared sexual images of you behind your back – were all too familiar. *How would I feel if I were in her shoes?* I was one of the few victims who'd secured a conviction for image-based sexual abuse.

At that time there were all manner of loopholes in the law through which perpetrators of image-based sexual abuse could escape prosecution. *Something needs to happen to change this*, I realised.

Government research shows that one in seven women and one in nine men aged between eighteen and thirty-four have experienced threats to share intimate images. And UK police recorded more than 28,000 reports of disclosing private sexual images without consent between April 2015 and December 2021.

It's staggering how many victims of this crime go unheard. Looking into the legal issues surrounding image-based sexual abuse, I met Kate Isaacs, who founded Not Your Porn, a campaign to make hosting non-consensual content illegal. She told me, 'Unfortunately, a lot of the victims I've worked with over the last three years haven't even got an arrest, let alone a conviction.'

Worryingly, even when victims do secure a conviction, the offending images remain online – because they're not deemed 'illegal content'. Often, victims must pay extortionate fees to huge tech companies to remove the pictures or footage. I'll be eternally grateful to online enforcement analyst Matthew Redden for not charging me when he removed my sex footage from PornHub – otherwise, that video of Bear and me would be easier to find online (it saddens me to say that it is still out there).

Recently, I appeared on *Good Morning Britain* (GMB) to comment on a landmark case that saw a woman awarded almost £100,000 in damages after her ex-partner, Stuart Gaunt, secretly filmed her naked in the shower – footage that then appeared on a porn website.

The victim, Victoria (not her real name) reported Gaunt to police. He got a suspended jail sentence for voyeurism but wasn't charged with putting the images online or ordered to take them down. So, Victoria took her case to the High Court where, in February 2023, she won the first case of damages for image-based sexual abuse in England and Wales. However, Victoria is still struggling to get the images removed because Gaunt took them and therefore owns copyright. The pictures of Victoria have been on the internet since 2017. I can't begin to imagine the distress this has caused her.

An actress relayed Victoria's horrific experience on the *GMB* feature. 'There's this weird thing: like, is this real? Did this really happen?' she said. 'You don't know because you're so accustomed to how that person is with you. So kind, so caring. Then, on the opposite you have the depravity of what is going on.'

From the *GMB* sofa, I said of Victoria's case, 'In my opinion, the perpetrator should have been tried for image-based sexual abuse. Presumably, as Victoria didn't know cams were filming, she probably didn't have any proof to show he [Gaunt] intended to cause distress. Whether or not a perpetrator intends to cause distress, it [the footage] actually does. It's an absolutely inhuman thing to do to another human being and it should be illegal no matter what. A lot of people are doing this for monetary gain.'

Gaunt's footage caused Victoria long-term distress. She told *GMB*, via the actress, that she now finds herself searching for hidden cameras in hotel rooms when she's away on business trips. 'I check the air-con vents – because the cameras are just so small . . . you don't know where they are.'

I strongly empathise with Victoria on this. I've struggled to trust men since Bear filmed me. Whenever I go on a date, I'm always on the lookout for hidden cameras. It's like a form of post-traumatic stress disorder. My body feels unsafe in certain situations. On one date, a boy started snogging me in a lift, which sent me into a panic. 'I'm sorry,' I said, 'I can't do this.' I was paranoid our kiss might be caught on CCTV and then distributed to the world. No one should be made to feel this way.

Bear didn't have to go to jail, and he could've avoided this punishment. If he'd admitted the charges, he probably would've got off with some community service. I still ask myself, *Why did Bear do this to me?* I hadn't done anything to upset him, so you could argue that there was no 'revenge' involved in my case. Maybe he just wanted to make money? Or maybe, as he said in court, he simply thought I'd find our video 'funny'. Oh, I could go on forever trying to get inside Bear's mind, but at the end of the day, only he knows why he put that video on porn sites.

Moving on with my life after Bear's conviction, I've learned so much about myself. I now think, *Maybe this situation was meant to happen to me?* Getting through the court case made me realise just how resilient I am.

In some ways, waiving my anonymity really brought me peace and love. I'm lucky to have the tools – a loving family, friends, and overwhelming support from the British public – to guide me through this challenging process.

Having open conversations about image-based sexual abuse has highlighted to me just how prevalent this crime is. I now know I have nothing to be ashamed of. The only people who should be ashamed are those who share explicit content without consent.

Being exposed in a sex tape could've crushed my soul, career and life, but somehow I managed to push through this experience – and, hopefully, this means thousands of other victims will win justice against the perpetrators of the crimes against them. Don't get me wrong, my experience was a nightmare, but I managed to turn that nightmare into something positive. My nightmare has brought me hope and resilience but, most importantly, it's given me a voice – and the power to help other victims of image-based sexual abuse.

This is not a shameful story – it's a journey to empowerment.

'YOU ARE ABSOLUTELY
PERFECT JUST BEING
YOU. DON'T TRY
TO BE ANYTHING
LESS THAN YOUR
AUTHENTIC SELF –
BECAUSE THAT IS THE
SEXIEST VERSION
OF YOURSELF.'

'OUR INNER
THOUGHTS AND
FEELINGS CONTROL
OUR OUTER REALITY.
STOP REACTING TO
YOUR OUTER WORLD
AND START WORKING
ON YOUR INNER
BEING. THAT IS WHEN
YOU WILL TRULY
SEE YOUR MAGIC.'

Chapter Six

TAKING BACK
MY BODY CONFIDENCE

The trolls are always going to troll, aren't they?

Amid the thousands upon thousands of supportive wishes that light up my social-media pages, some people will occasionally try to stick the knife in.

Thankfully, there are only a handful of hateful lurkers. They usually crawl out of the woodwork whenever I post about my campaigning work on image-based sexual abuse. They'll write shit like, *You're half naked in your pictures on here [Instagram], so does it really matter at this point?* Or, *Get a proper job, you bimbo.*

What are they saying? That I'm a hypocrite for displaying pictures of myself in a bikini or gym gear after being exploited in a sex tape, filmed and posted on porn sites without my consent? What do they expect? For me to walk around in a morphsuit for the rest of my life, just because I'm a victim of revenge porn? Absolutely not. I don't rise or reply to these comments on my social platforms. I choose to post my pictures, but I didn't agree to my sex life being cruelly exposed online. So, my message to the trolls is this: get over it. We should be able to celebrate our bodies and beauty in whichever way we wish – and feel safe to do so. End of.

I believe we should love and nourish our bodies from the inside out. Nowadays, fitness, health and mental wellbeing hold the key to my happiness and confidence. But it's taken me a while to learn to love the body God gifted me with. Trust me, like many other women and girls out there, I've had a few physical hang-ups over the years.

My body insecurities started when I was around twelve. As I've previously mentioned, I suffered from acute psoriasis for many years. Psoriasis is an autoimmune skin disorder, usually brought on by stress and hormonal changes. Unhealthy habits such as smoking or boozing too much can also trigger psoriasis. My condition was really bad; I was literally covered in flaky, raised spots of pink and white skin. I tried to cover up the patches with foundation sprays or concealer, but this only made it look worse. Thick dust would seep through my nude tights and tumble from my scalp, covering my school blazer in skin confetti. The school bullies would point at my arms or face or legs and, with their faces scrunched up in disgust, say, 'What the fuck is wrong with your skin?' I'd try to laugh off their offensive comments. I'd say, 'Yeah, I've been eaten alive by gnats,' or make up some other lie, but this bullying really affected my mental health.

One episode remains clear in my mind. It happened on a Thursday afternoon after school, inside the Subway sandwich shop on Loughton High Road. Aged thirteen, I was so chuffed to have been invited there by Susan and Charlene, who were the most popular girls in the year above me. Imagine: I'm strutting into Subway thinking, This is wicked. I'm out with the cool girls. Yeah, I've really made it in life. Then I got super excited when we bumped into a group of older boys from our school, who invited us girls to join them at their table. So we sat down with our food and fizzy drinks, and the boys were like, 'Y'alright?' to Charlene and Susan. I sat there drinking my Diet Coke, still feeling pretty smug. And I think I just said something like, 'How's it going?' when the boys burst out laughing.

Todd, the boy sitting opposite me, put down his meatball sandwich and elbowed his mate (I can't remember his name) in the ribs. 'Look boys, it's Hell Girl,' he said, with a grin too big for his fucking face.

'Yeah, show us your horns, Crusty,' said his mate, prompting another chorus of laughter. Even Susan and Charlene were laughing now. 'Hell Girl' was another nickname for me – because I had two massive red patches on my forehead that looked like scars from where my devil 'horns' had snapped off, apparently.

I stared down at my hands, then quickly shoved them into my lap; they were encrusted in psoriasis too. My eyes burned with tears as the sniggering engulfed me like an itchy, heavy blanket. 'Oi, what's up, Scabby?' That was Todd again. Every inch of my skin prickled; I could feel more psoriasis joining the patchwork party on my body in response to those cruel remarks. I had to get out of there before I started full-on crying at the table. My chair screamed as its legs skidded backwards across the vinyl floor and I shot up and flew out of Subway. I ran to the bus stop, sobbing for Essex, for Britain, for the fucking world, because I honestly felt like the ugliest girl on the planet. I cried for the entire bus journey home, the names 'Hell Girl' and 'Crusty' and 'Scabby' scoring deep gashes through my head and heart. The next day, I felt too traumatised and humiliated to go to school. I couldn't face seeing Todd and his mates, or Susan and Charlene. In the end, I did go to school, the scars from where my 'horns' once lived caked in make-up, fresh patches weaving a bloody tapestry over my arms and legs. And so the cycle continued: the bullies called me names, which exacerbated my psoriasis, and I'd get more and more upset.

Mum took me to the hospital all the time for my psoriasis, asking skin specialists, 'What new steroid creams are there?' and 'Could light therapy be an option?' or 'Are there any drugs for psoriasis?' Every time, I'd pray that the next remedy I tried would cure my skin disease. In retrospect, the question *I* should have asked to myself is, 'Which emotions are causing my psoriasis?' I wasn't entirely happy in my early teens; steroid creams did occasionally ease my condition, but those ointments couldn't dampen my stress or insecurities, which were causing the problem in the first place. My psoriasis plagued me through my late teens and early twenties. I smoked cigarettes and probably poured too much alcohol down my throat back then. My diet wasn't the best either, composed of a fair amount of fast food and meat. So, in later years, I decided to change my eating habits, to slow down and enjoy some peace in my life. By changing my diet and mindset – I went vegan for six weeks and took up yoga and meditation – my skin improved.

I don't think there's one person on this earth who doesn't remember a traumatic experience from their childhood. But, as I've found, if you're able to reframe those bad childhood memories in your mind, then you gain confidence as an adult. Being bullied was traumatic for me. Todd and his mates made me feel worthless, a lesser human being, just because I had a skin condition. I now realise those bullies were simply projecting their insecurities on me to make themselves feel better.

Thankfully, I'm now psoriasis-free, but if it were to flare up again, I'd talk about it. I'd tell people outright: 'I have psoriasis. It's an autoimmune skin condition that's largely caused by stress.' I know I'm not alone, either. So many celebrities and influencers are having open conversations about the condition. I applaud Kim Kardashian for publicly sharing her journey with psoriasis and psoriatic arthritis. And good on model and actress Cara Delevingne, who chose to expose her 'stress-related' sores on the red carpet at the 2022 Met Gala. As she told *Glamour* magazine: 'At first, I was like, "Wait a minute, I should cover this up, right?" and then I remembered, though, that it's not good for my skin and a lot of people live with psoriasis.'

I wholeheartedly agree with Cara. Living with a skin disease doesn't change who you are as a person.

As a teenage schoolkid, I didn't worry about my figure or what I ate. From the age of fifteen, I was around a size ten, with quite big boobs, I suppose. I don't recall ever thinking, *I could do with losing a few pounds* or *If only I had thinner thighs*. Fast-forward three years, throw in a toxic relationship, and I suddenly developed body-image issues.

In an earlier chapter of this book, I mentioned Shane, an ex-boyfriend. To recap, Shane was everything I was looking for in a relationship when we first got together. He showered me with compliments and always called or messaged me when he said he would. We fancied each other like crazy in those early days, but just weeks into our relationship, Shane's behaviour switched dramatically. That's when he started mentally and physically abusing me.

Shane's verbal abuse triggered my body dysmorphia. 'You're fat,' he said one day as we lay naked in bed, just after we'd had sex. 'You might look all right when you're dressed, but with your clothes off, you're disgusting.' Another time, Shane threw a glass of orange juice in my face and growled, 'You're not pretty'. I felt so ashamed.

I convinced myself, *Shane's right; you're disgusting. Everyone else must think you're disgusting too.* Then I told myself, *You have to do something about this. Lose a bit of weight – then people will think you're beautiful.* So, I cut down my food intake. Initially, I'd skip meals here and there, but soon I was barely eating anything. I didn't even notice my rapid weight loss because, in my head, I was still unattractive. Even after I'd finished with Shane I continued to obsess about my looks. I had zero energy, my hair started to thin, and, in retrospect, I looked bloody terrible. It scares the shit out of me now to look back at some of the pap pictures taken of me in those days. My legs were teeny as I stumbled out of yet another nightclub or bar. When those photographs appeared on news sites like MailOnline, I'd get trolled for being *too skinny*. In one picture, taken after a security guard had to carry me out of a nightclub in Soho, my skin looked pure pigeon-grey. One commenter on that image asked, *Is she a heroin addict?* Meanwhile, some friends nicknamed me '2D Gee'. 'You're so skinny we can't see you,' they'd say. Yet I still couldn't see how thin I'd become. Fainting in the street one day should have served as a wake-up call that my body was crying out for nourishment.

Mum, always my rock in life, finally brought me to my senses regarding my weight one Christmas Day. 'Georgia, sweetie, I'm so worried about you,' she said as I sat next to her at the dinner table, party hat sliding down to my eyes over my thinning hair, feigning interest in the uneaten but delicious meal before me. She winged her arm around my thin shoulders, her voice loaded with concern but, as always, non-judgemental. 'I want you to come upstairs with me, Georgia. I think we should get you on the scales. You've lost a lot of weight, and that's not healthy. Please, sweetie, let me help you.'

I dropped my fork and looked at Mum. 'Okay,' I said. Inside, I knew she was right. We went up to the bathroom and I stepped onto the scales, Mum watching over my shoulder as the needle slowly swished to just over seven stone on the display. I'd been a healthy nine-and-a-half stone before. 'Shit, I had no idea I'd lost this much weight,' I said. 'I'd better get some hot dinners down my neck. Sorry, Mum, I didn't mean to worry you.'

Mum kissed my head. 'It's okay, sweetie. You've had a few struggles lately, but we're going to get through this. I'm going to help you. You're beautiful, inside and out. Never let anyone tell you otherwise.'

I thanked her and we went downstairs – and I ate a big chunk of Christmas pudding.

Fortunately, I acknowledged that I was slightly underweight. Thanks to my ever-supportive family and friends, I managed to come back fighting fit from that episode. Although I didn't have a diagnosed eating disorder, I was so traumatised from Shane's abuse that I didn't have much of an appetite. Gradually, my relationship with food improved and I returned to a healthy weight again. I ate nutritious meals and went to the gym every day. It felt so amazing to get my energy back.

However, while I felt healthier, I still battled with my body image in my relationships. I mean, no girl wants to be told they look disgusting, do they? Shane's remarks lingered in my mind; I took my body insecurities into my next partnership, with Jake. Whenever he said lovely things about my figure or looks, I'd find myself dismissing his compliments with retorts like, 'Shut up, I'm not pretty. I don't even like looking at myself in the mirror.'

I remember one evening, as Jake and I were getting ready to go out for a meal, he told me I looked stunning, or something similar. 'No, I don't. I look rough,' I said, the words naturally slipping from my mouth.

Jake, exasperated, grabbed my hand and dragged me over to the full-length mirror in my bedroom. 'Look at yourself, will you?' he said, positioning me in front of the glass. He stood behind me, his reflection meeting mine in the mirror, and lightly brushed the back of his hand over my cheek. 'You're fucking beautiful,' he said, kissing my neck. 'You don't realise how beautiful you are.'

That moment meant everything to me. Granted, I didn't look at myself and think, *Yeah, you're well pretty*, but Jake had made me *feel* beautiful. No man had said such loving words to me before. I'll always remember that scene in the mirror with Jake as the moment I began to reclaim my self-confidence as a woman.

My aim in this book is to be downright honest. I want you to know the real me, to feel as though I'm chatting to you as a friend. That's why I'm writing about cosmetic surgery.

As we all know, celebrities are often called out in the press for their surgical 'enhancements'. You know the kind of thing I mean: has this celeb taken things too far with her latest bum enlargement, boob augmentation, fillers or Botox job? I firmly believe women shouldn't feel pressured by society to go under the knife – or risk their health by doing so. The Brazilian Butt Lift (BBL), for example, is the world's most dangerous cosmetic procedure. The surgeon extracts fat from various parts of your body, then injects that fat into your arse. Women have died on the operating table from botched surgeries. Some of my friends have had BBLs, and while I don't judge anyone who undergoes this procedure, I would never consider getting a bum lift. But I'm not averse to surgical enhancements in moderation – especially if the procedures are for medical purposes or simply to boost your confidence. At the end of the day, I think cosmetic surgery is all about being responsible, and I'm not going to bullshit you: I've had a little work done myself.

My boobs changed drastically following my weight loss. Even when I put weight on again, they didn't return to how they used to be. Seriously, my breasts resembled deflated udders. One boob sagged to the right and the other shot left; they looked like they were having a row with each other. My nipples had gone flat and would only pop out if I was cold or horny. I didn't feel comfortable in a bikini and uplifting bras didn't do much lifting in my case as my skin had lost its elasticity. I lived with my flaccid boobs for almost five years before deciding, in September 2020, to do something about them.

I told the Harley Street surgeon Dr Riccardo Frati, 'I don't want huge beach balls – please can you give me the smallest tits possible?' I wanted my boob job to look natural and in proportion to the rest of my body. Dr Frati was a genius. Once the bandages came off and the swelling subsided, I was left with the most natural-looking, 220cc-sized ('cc' represents cubic centimetres) boobs.

I was thrilled with them; I couldn't thank the surgeon enough.

Getting my boobs done was definitely the right decision for me. I've undergone a few other procedures too, which I've spoken publicly about. In November 2021, I had a second operation to fix my deviated septum. My first rhinoplasty op went wrong, so I got Dr Frati to sort my nose out this time. Unlike my boob procedure, my nose surgery wasn't for cosmetic reasons. I'd broken my nose as a kid while messing about with some friends. I was lying on the floor of a train and my mate, who had a broken arm at the time, went to lift me up. As she tried to help me to my feet, I tripped and smacked my nose on a hand pole, resulting in my deviated septum. I vlogged about my nose surgery, explaining to my followers why I hadn't mentioned the previous op, which I underwent immediately after I filmed *Love Island*. At that time, I'd feared being trolled for 'getting a nose job'. 'Now I'm twenty-six, I feel more confident to talk about this issue,' I said in my vlog.

A few months before my nose surgery, I also vlogged about my decision to have lip-filler injections. Being a reality-TV star means companies offer you procedures such as this on the house – and, I admit, I took this opportunity too far. My lips looked ridiculous after too many dermal injections – I had that dinghy look going on. Eventually, I got the fillers dissolved and my lips returned to their natural shape, but I still go for tiny filler enhancements now and then. Big lips are so last season.

*

I've never viewed myself as a famous person, not in the celebrity sense, anyway. It took me a while to adapt to my reality-television 'fame'. Initially, I'd be surprised when people recognised me in the street and asked me to pose for selfies with them. I always oblige as I feel so humbled when they say stuff like, 'I thought you were brilliant on *Love Island*'. It's my absolute pleasure to smile in pictures with the people who support my career. So, when a woman approached me for a picture opportunity outside the L'Opera nightclub in Saint-Tropez in summer 2020, I was like, 'Yeah, bring it on.'

I was holidaying in the French Riviera with my best mates Tyla and Star at the time. We were all a bit tipsy – actually, I was pretty smashed now I think of it – after a night on the cocktails in L'Opera. I was wearing a white trouser suit, the left leg of it pushed up to my knee as I sat on the kerb to take off one of my spiky heels, Tyla and Star standing over me, giggling. That's when the woman came up to me. She seemed lovely: thirtyish and oh so polite, with a camera hanging on a strap around her neck. *Probably some random port photographer*, I thought.

'Hi, have you had a good night?' she asked.

I lifted my stiletto sandal above my head to confirm, 'yes'.

'Ah, glad to hear it. Listen, would you like me to take some photographs of you and your friends?'

'God, yeah, that'll be great. Where d'ya want me?' I put on my shoe and reached for Tyla's hand, cutting a gibbon-like stance as I stood – arms out, knees bent and splayed, my left trouser leg still rolled up – while the woman snapped away and said nice things about my outfit. Amused by this situation, I said, 'Let's do some shots over there.' I flung my hand to indicate the harbour ahead, lined with glittering superyachts. The camerawoman was well up for this, which egged me on further. I cut a wobbly path to the harbourside and lay down on the pavement, pulling silly poses. One second, I was on my back, legs in the air; the next, on my stomach, shouting, 'Is this okay?' Tyla and Star joined in, although they stayed on their feet, making 'ta-da' gestures with their arms. We were all killing ourselves laughing. I wanted to carry on but after a few minutes, the woman said she had to leave. 'Lovely to meet you,' I said as she hurried off along the harbour clutching her camera.

The next day, those pictures of me, Tyla and Star appeared on MailOnline – as well as other shots of us staggering back to our hotel. The headline read: Love Island's *Georgia Harrison looks very worse for wear as bleary-eyed star stumbles out of nightclub and rolls around on the ground in Saint-Tropez.* I found this hilarious. Tyla and Star were like, 'We're famous.' The camerawoman was obviously a pap who'd secretly followed us after she'd pretended to leave. I had to laugh. This wasn't the first time I'd been photographed looking 'worse for wear'. Getting papped goes with the territory of being in the public eye. You've got to take the highs with the lows in this game.

That said, there was a time when I did let my body insecurities get the better of me on Instagram. Shortly after I appeared on *Love Island*, I fell into the trap of wanting to look perfect in my pictures, so I edited them slightly. Nipped my waist a little in some photographs and made my bum curvier in others. But after a few months, I realised that what I was doing was wrong. After educating myself on the negative impact my editing could have on my followers, I decided to address the issue head-on. I posted the following message to those I'd misguided:

> *I'm sorry for making my insecurities your insecurities.*
>
> *I haven't been over-editing my photos for a long time now and although I learnt my lesson, I never really took accountability for the fact that I did it.*
>
> *I'm sorry to myself for not loving my imperfections the way I encourage others to. And I'm sorry to society for once being part of the problem.*
>
> *I promise to continue to embrace my authentic self going forwards and I acknowledge that authenticity is the highest form of love for oneself and others.*

I stand by those words – I really do regret trying to be somebody other than my authentic self, and, once again, I apologise for my mistake.

Today, my attitude towards food and appearances is far more positive. I've learned to respect my body by giving it the nutrition, fitness and peace it deserves. For a long while I looked at food in a negative way. I'd think, *If I eat that pizza or bowl of pasta, I'll put on loads of weight.* Now, I think of food in a loving way. I eat healthily – I love vegetables, juices and fish – but I'll also demolish a pizza if I fancy one. Again, everything in moderation. We're so lucky to live in a society where we can just pick up a phone, touch the screen and have whatever food we want delivered to our doorsteps.

Fitness is very important to me, too, and I like to vary my exercise routine, from HIIT workouts and body-pump classes to running and yoga, which I'm really into right now. I'm a huge fan of Bikram yoga, which involves holding concentrated poses inside a heated room. It's great for your posture while cleansing your body and mind of all toxins. I can go into a Bikram class really hungover and come skipping out ninety minutes later.

Throughout my spiritual journey, I've also learned that attraction doesn't boil down to how skinny, curvy or pretty you are. It's about being present in the room and believing in yourself, in your soul. When it comes to attraction, humans have an extra awareness that goes beyond the five senses. I believe that we all have an aura, and are connected in ways that can't be seen by the naked eye. We give off vibes and our auras attract people to us. A positive attitude feeds our auras; the more we see the best in ourselves, the more attractive we become. Sometimes our insecurities are buried so deep in our subconscious that we don't even realise we're constantly putting ourselves down in our thoughts.

I think most women don't realise how beautiful they are. We girls often put a tonne of effort into getting dressed up for a night out – then spend the entire evening wondering why nobody's reacting to how we look. I should know, I've been in this situation hundreds of times. If you're always thinking that you look fat, or your hair looks rubbish, then you're projecting unattractive energy.

The other day, I went out in a little spiritual jumpsuit, with no make-up on, and lots of people told me how good I looked. By not giving a shit, I believe I gave off positive vibes that attracted those people to me.

It can be difficult to supress our body insecurities, especially when we put pressure on ourselves to look perfect. But negative thoughts will hold you back from being the most authentic and magnetic version of yourself. Therefore, I highly recommend you try this: for one night, why don't you and your mate walk into a public space, be it a bar, café, party or whatever, and just practice not giving a fuck? Dedicate that time to yourselves, concentrate on the people around you, and let go of any insecure thoughts. And if you do feel negative thoughts creeping into your mind, like, *My hair looks crap* or whatever, counteract those thoughts with positive ones. All you need to do is use your eyes, ears, mouth and nose and connect with people. I can guarantee those people will react differently to you. As I say to my followers, 'You are absolutely perfect just being you. Don't try to be anything less than your authentic self – because that is the sexiest version of yourself.'

'THIS TOO SHALL PASS.'

A Persian adage

'LET YOUR BROKEN
HEART BE FREE
TO WEEP AS IT
PROCESSES THE
THINGS IT'S LEFT
BEHIND BUT, WHEN
THE TIME IS RIGHT,
MAY IT HEAL BIGGER
THAN EVER, LEAVING
MAGICAL SPACE FOR
THE ENERGY OF
SOMETHING NEW.'

Chapter Seven

TAKING BACK
MY GRIEF

LOUGHTON, ESSEX,
LATE NOVEMBER 2021

I was in M&S Simply Food buying ingredients for a roast dinner when Cenk Fahri, my best boy-mate in the world, FaceTimed me.

His face filled my phone screen, washed in blueish light. He was smiling as always, but he didn't sound like himself when he started talking. Cenk usually booms and laughs down the phone in a voice like a carnival. Today, he sounded a bit flat. 'All right, Gee, what're you up to?'

I turned around and angled my phone so he could see the chickens in the fridge behind me. 'I'm buying loads of stuff for a roast,' I said, laughing. 'I'm trying to get myself a boyfriend. I'm gonna learn how to make a roast dinner and put it all on my Instagram. Y'know, get a bit of clickbait to let the boys know I'm wifey material.' I laughed and made my way into the next aisle to look for stuffing. 'Anyway, what are you up to? Where are you?'

Cenk rolled his lips inwards between his teeth, blinked a few times. 'Ah, I'm in an ambulance . . . going to the hospital. It's not looking good, Gee,' he said.

My throat tightened. Cenk had been battling leukaemia for the last ten years. In that time, he'd survived rounds of gruelling chemo but enjoyed long stretches in remission. His cancer had since returned. This time, doctors had diagnosed Cenk with acute lymphoblastic leukaemia, an aggressive cancer that affects your white blood cells, and predicted he had only six months to live.

But he'd seemed slightly better lately. I'd set up a GoFundMe page, which had raised almost £60,000 to pay for a nutritionist and holistic therapies for Cenk. He'd responded well to these treatments; the number of cancer cells in his body had dropped. We'd all been praying for a miracle, especially as Cenk was such a fighter. Now, sadness and helplessness welled in his eyes.

'I'll tell you what, Cenk. When you get home, I'm gonna make you a roast dinner too,' I said, trying to be positive, but Cenk was crying now, and I could feel my bottom lip going. *Don't cry, be upbeat, for Cenk.* 'You'll love it.'

Cenk sniffed hard. 'Gee, I don't think I'll ever get to have a roast with you,' he said. 'I don't think I'm coming home. Not this time. I don't think I'll ever see you again, Gee.'

'Don't be silly. Don't say things like that. What happened to being positive?' I'd never seen Cenk like this before. Even when he was going through hardcore chemo, he'd push on with sheer positivity and determination. He never complained about his illness – he was more interested in other people than himself.

'Why has God done this to me, Gee? What have I done in my life to deserve this? What am I being punished for?'

I wanted to be there with him, to hug him. I wanted to make his leukaemia go away. Nobody loved life more than Cenk, but standing there in M&S, tears now streaking my face, I had a horrible feeling that Cenk was saying goodbye to me. I put down my basket and touched his sweet face on the screen. 'Cenk, you are the best, most magnificent soul I have ever met. If anyone's getting punished, there'll be many who'll drop before you,' I said. 'Mate, I'll probably go before you – because you're so special. You're going to be absolutely fine. You're going to come home – just like you always do.'

'I'm not sure I will come home this time.' Cenk wiped his eyes on the sleeve of his jacket. 'I love you, Gee.'

'Well, you must come home because I love you so much. I just can't imagine my life without you.'

Cenk's mouth quivered into a smile, then he pulled back his head and laughed. He looked more like himself again. 'Yeah, you're right. I've bought too many fucking expensive clothes to die yet.'

I laughed too, through the heavy, dragging grief pains in my chest that told me, *This* is *goodbye*, and said, 'I know, right. You didn't spend all that fucking money in Gucci for nothing, mate.'

I told Cenk I loved him again and we ended our call. Suddenly, my enthusiasm for cooking disappeared, but I still bought the ingredients anyway, telling myself, *Cenk wants you to cook this roast dinner.* When I got home, I sent a voice note to the girls on our WhatsApp chat group. I explained my conversation with Cenk. 'I'm sure he was trying to say goodbye to me,' I said, but my friends said, 'We've spoken to him too and he's going to be all right. He's probably just a bit low about going back into hospital.'

God, how I hoped the girls were right. But Cenk was my soulmate – I knew him inside and out. For the last ten years he'd been saying, 'I'm fine, I'm not ill.' Today, even when he'd joked about his clothes, I'd sensed the abject fear in his soul.

I cried as I fumbled around in Mum's kitchen that Sunday afternoon, dropping Yorkshire puddings on the floor and burning the gravy. I couldn't get my earlier conversation with Cenk out of my head. *Cenk can't die. He's only twenty-seven.* As I'd said to him earlier, I couldn't imagine my life without him.

Cenk and I had been best mates since we first met in 2006. Already, we'd shared so many happy – and sad – moments together. During our schooldays, Cenk and I lived opposite one another in Buckhurst Hill. We'd literally spend every day together back then. I'd be sitting in the lounge watching TV when Cenk's little head would pop around the back door. 'Hey, can I come in? I've brought snacks,' he'd say. Ha ha, Cenk always had a big bag of sweets or crisps or Greggs Yum Yum doughnuts on the go. Skinny as a rake, despite eating like a horse. Then we'd sit on the sofa for hours, scoffing snacks, chatting and laughing. Always laughing.

Honestly, you couldn't meet a lovelier boy than Cenk. Caring and considerate, with a cheeky handsomeness, I used to say to him, 'Cenk, you're every parent's dream son.'

I'll never forget the day Cenk called me in 2011 and said, 'Gee, I've gotta tell you something.' I was abroad visiting my dad at the time, I recall. From Cenk's opening line I guessed he was about to tell me something serious, like, maybe one of his grandparents had died? But what he said next knocked me sideways, 'I've got leukaemia . . . cancer, Gee.'

From that moment I was beside myself, howling, choking, almost hyperventilating. 'No, Cenk, please no.' I never thought I'd hear such devastating news from a best friend.

'It's okay, chill out,' said Cenk. 'I'm young. Lots of people my age get cancer – and the odds of survival are okay.' I was inconsolable after that call, sobbing my eyes out in Dad's garden, thinking, *It's not fair. How can something so cruel happen to such a decent, beautiful and kind human being?*

I had to be strong, though, for Cenk and his family. Cenk would literally do anything for me, so the least I could do was be there to give him my love and support as he faced this shattering news.

Being so popular – everybody adored Cenk – he had a solid friendship network around him, so he was never short of visitors during his spells in hospital. Some days, about twenty of us would go up there to see him, armed with burger or lobster meals and Cenk's favourite snacks. We'd take over the kids' cancer ward, where Cenk, then seventeen, was the oldest patient.

Often, I stayed overnight at the hospital with him, particularly when he was undergoing chemotherapy sessions. I'd push my bed next to Cenk's so I could cuddle him from behind while we watched television. We were like naughty kids on a sleepover, whispering and giggling and never turning off the TV at lights-out time, when the nurse would come over and wag her finger in our faces. 'I've told you two before,' she'd say. 'Cenk, if you want Georgia to stay over then you must turn the television off and go to sleep when I ask.' Cenk and I would mumble our apologies before giggling again.

Bless Cenk, he laughed and smiled through every round of his cancer treatment. His resilience knew no bounds, even though he obviously experienced a great deal of pain and discomfort. I remember waking up with him during the night following his chemo sessions, and he'd be like a furnace. 'I'm just a bit hot,' he'd say, so I'd tiptoe along to the little kitchen off the ward, grab a few cans of Coke from the fridge, then take them back to bed to roll over Cenk's burning skin.

Over the next few years, Cenk recovered from leukaemia three times after enduring a host of invasive procedures, including a bone-marrow transplant (luckily, his brother was a perfect donor match) and CAR T-cell therapy. We thought he'd be cancer-free for the foreseeable future; following the success of those treatments, Cenk had transformed his diet and had been able to maintain a healthy and happy life – until November 2021.

Almost three months before I received Cenk's phone call in M&S, his oncologist had told him there was nothing else the hospital could do for him aside from providing pain management. I can't even begin to imagine how Cenk must've felt when the oncologist gave him a life-expectancy of only six months. But the first thing he did after hearing that tragic news was to help another person in need. As he walked out of the hospital, he came across an elderly man who'd fallen over in the street. The man was disorientated, so Cenk stayed with him for over an hour and somehow – I don't know the full details – he managed to find the man's family. His actions at that incredibly challenging time fully reflect Cenk: selfless and kind-hearted beyond belief. Through and through.

After our FaceTime call, Cenk went into hospital, but I couldn't visit him as he didn't want his friends seeing him while he was so poorly.

I next spoke to Cenk on the evening of 12 December, my birthday, when his mum FaceTimed me from the hospital. She said he was in a bad way, that he hadn't been able to speak all day, but wanted to wish me happy birthday. Then she handed the phone to Cenk, who was propped up in his hospital bed, connected to wires and tubes. Oh, he looked so pale and thin. 'Hey Gee, happy birthday. I love you,' he said between gasps in a voice like crunching autumn leaves.

'Thanks, Cenk,' I said, swallowing my tears. 'I love you too. So fucking much.'

'What did you do today?' rasped Cenk, and I had to think on my feet. Truth was, I hadn't felt like celebrating my birthday. Not without Cenk. Instead, I'd gone to church with my mum and her sister, Aunty Sharon, and my mates Rachel, Bella, Tyla and Star to pray for him. Again, we'd prayed for a miracle to happen.

'Oh, we went for a meal and a few drinks. Nothing major,' I said.

Cenk could barely breathe now, but he winked and wished me a happy birthday again. I blew him a big kiss. 'I love you, Cenk. Speak soon.' Those were the last words I said to my dearest friend.

Nine days later, on Tuesday 21 December 2021, I woke up full of energy. I thought, *Twenty-one, twenty-one, that's a positive number.* Lately, I'd been doing some spiritual talks on social media, but I'd found myself getting a bit tongue-tied and blocked during those videos. For some reason, this didn't happen today. I was really feeling the energy, you know? I put on a yellow hat and posted a short video, urging my followers to have faith in the universe and such, then I headed out in the car with Sky, ready for our morning walk. As I turned out of our street, my phone rang. I pulled over to take the call from my friend Reiss's mum, Cheryl. Reiss and Cenk had been best mates since childhood. 'Hi, Georgia,' said Cheryl, 'Cenk's gone.'

'Gone where?' I asked, 'home?'

'No, sadly not. Cenk passed away this morning. He's at peace now.'

I couldn't speak for a few seconds; although I'd been expecting this news, it still hit me like a train. *Cenk, gone? He couldn't just vanish. He didn't just die, did he?* I swallowed hard. Sky whimpered in the passenger seat. I broke down. 'Thanks for letting me know, Cheryl,' I said, then hung up and cried, as Mariah Carey's 'All I Want for Christmas is You' came on the radio. *Twenty-one, twenty-one. This will always be Cenk's number.*

I called Mum and my friends from the car. 'Cenk passed away this morning,' I said. I didn't want them to hear this news from anyone but me. Then I drove to Tyla and Star's house. They were in bits too. We cried and hugged and looked at photographs of us with Cenk on our phones. 'I can't believe he's gone,' we all kept saying. I posted a message on Instagram, along with a video clip of Cenk, kissing me on the cheek, set to the soundtrack of 'Dancing in the Sky' by twin Canadian singers, Dani and Lizzy. I'd heard the song, written by Lizzy after her friend died, on TikTok a couple of weeks before. It's a sad but beautiful song, asking whether a loved one's fear and pain has vanished with their passing. I hoped Cenk was dancing in the sky as I wrote my message, inviting his friends to the Warren Wood pub in Buckhurst Hill to: *try and drink to his life.* In tribute to Cenk, I added, in pink text: *I'm so grateful for everything, and as much as it kills me to let you go, I feel blessed to have had a best friend as amazing, funny, loyal, positive, handsome, charismatic, and everything more as you. I truly hope you're dancing in the sky like we used to. I'll always be dancing with you in my heart, Cenky.*

That afternoon, around three hundred people gathered to remember Cenk. The Warren Wood was Cenk's favourite pub – he was part of the furniture there. I was an emotional wreck, tears gushing uncontrollably down my face in front of everyone. Occasionally, somebody would bring me round with a funny Cenk anecdote, then I'd be off again, sobbing into my wine. We drank all afternoon and into the evening. I smoked cigarettes for the first time in years, consumed by grief, panic, shock and disbelief. By 8 p.m., I couldn't stand up. My mates Bella and Jordan had to carry me home.

I was bereft without Cenk. He'd appreciated life more than anyone I've ever met. It broke my heart when Cenk's mum told me about his final moments in London's University College Hospital.

Before Cenk died he asked his mum if he could go outside. 'I just want to see the world one last time,' he said. Sadly, he couldn't go outside as he was too weak, but his mum wheeled him over to the window so he could see the world from his hospital room. He sat in his wheelchair for a few minutes, gazing at the view over London with a smile on his face, then said, 'I'm done now, Mum. Thank you.' This memory will haunt me forever. Cenk knew he was about to leave, and he wanted to look at the world – the world he fucking loved – for one last time. I can't think of a better example than this to make us appreciate how precious our lives are. We must own every day. 'Cenk passed away with a big smile on his face,' his mum told me. I made a promise to myself when she told me this: *I'll smile as much as I can.*

The days following Cenk's death were horrific. On Christmas Day, I could hardly eat anything. I sat at the dinner table, crying as I thought about my life with Cenk compared with my life without him. During the last few years in which he'd been well, we'd made so many happy memories. We'd travelled to Ibiza and Bali together, where we'd marvelled at glorious sunsets and star-studded skies over piña coladas. Cenk had always been like one of the girls, too. He loved a good gossip and comforted me through my heartbreaks. We'd never been romantically involved, but we did once make a pact to have a baby together if we were both 'still on the shelf' at thirty. I remember a discussion we once had when Cenk was in hospital. I was telling him how I'd like to have kids one day. 'The way I'm going, I'm gonna need a sperm donor,' I'd joked.

'They've got my sperm in a freezer here,' said Cenk. 'You can have that.' But this never happened because Cenk died before we could get anything confirmed in writing.

After Christmas dinner, I crawled back into bed, memories of Cenk whirling in my head. *Will I ever get over losing him?*

The turnout at Cenk's funeral was a testament to how

popular he was. There were at least four hundred people at the service, which was held in a mosque (Cenk's family are Muslim). His family hired Rolls-Royce cars for the funeral procession, and I travelled in one of them with Tyla and Star. There were tears, but also laughter as we celebrated Cenk's life and recalled our memories of him. After the burial, we all returned to the Warren Wood pub, where we released hundreds of white, biodegradable balloons, emblazoned with, *Forever in our hearts you'll stay. We will love you and remember you every single day*, into the rainy sky. I made a speech, which was so hard. I spoke about our special friendship, relaying memories of our conversations and fun moments over the years, adding, 'Cenk was handsome, funny, generous and kind. He always saw the magic in every moment – and he dressed so fucking well. His aura lit up a room.

'From this moment, I swear to love every moment in my life so much harder – in honour of him. To love more, dance more, worry less, stare at the stars, and savour every Yum Yum that enters my mouth.

'I'll feel stronger through every second of doubt along my path, knowing that I now have an angel forever in my heart, giving me the strength to overcome any setbacks and tribulations that I encounter.

'You were an absolute inspiration, and I will love and miss you for the rest of my life.'

I wanted to be happy – because I knew Cenk would hate for me to be sad – but I was grief-stricken. I felt like a widow. I had a complete breakdown inside the pub. *This is only the beginning of this grief journey*, I thought, as my friends carried me home again.

I'd never experienced raw grief like this. I'd seen Mum go through it when her mum, Jean, died suddenly in 2009. Of course, I'd grieved too then – I loved my nan, and she adored me – but it was a different kind of heartache. I was fourteen when Nan passed away. She'd gone into hospital with a water infection and then died later that day. She was in her sixties. I remember feeling guilty after Nan died, thinking I should have visited or called her more often. Mum was in a really bad state of grief though – totally inconsolable for months, which was understandable; she was as close with Nan as she is with me.

Getting through the weeks after Cenk's passing was incredibly tough, I won't lie. But I also knew I had to live my life to the full, for him. He wouldn't want to see me crying all the time. I embraced the spiritual moments in which I connected with him. Even now, whenever I see the number twenty-one, I immediately feel Cenk's energy, like he's here and telling me how to respond to certain situations.

On the morning of Cenk's funeral, an unusual-looking bug, black with red dots on its wings, landed on my arm. I brushed the insect away, but a couple of hours later, the bug reappeared on the rim of a candle jar in my bedroom. I cupped the insect in my hands and let it fly out of the window, thinking, *This is a sign from Cenk that everything's going to be okay.*

Don't get me wrong, I still had my bad days. Days when

I couldn't get out of bed in the morning for feeling so low. Some days, I wouldn't get up at all. I'd stay in bed, looking at photographs of Cenk on my phone, scrolling through old messages we'd exchanged, wishing I could be in this world, with him, even if only for one last time.

January slumped drearily into February, which brought more anxiety my way. On top of processing my emotions for Cenk, I also faced my revenge porn fight against Stephen Bear in court on 7 February. When Bear's trial was postponed until December – because his defence team needed 'more time' to prepare his case – it sent me into a tailspin of despair. I just wanted the trial over and done with so I could try to heal from the trauma of it all. The one person I wanted to speak to when I found out Bear's trial had been pushed back was Cenk. He'd been a pillar of strength throughout my sex-tape ordeal. Cenk thought Bear was a scumbag. 'I don't understand why you fancied him in the first place,' he'd said not long after Bear's arrest. 'But look, Gee, you're such a good person and he's definitely gonna get his karma. You just need to be strong.' I replayed Cenk's encouraging words in my mind whenever I felt stressed about the upcoming case, knowing he was with me in spirit.

Not a day passed that I didn't think about Cenk, but as the months progressed and I acknowledged the five stages of grief – denial, anger, bargaining, depression and acceptance – I slowly began to heal a little by channelling my grief through meditation and exercise. I started to get out and about more often with friends too. At the end of June, I went to Glastonbury Festival, and, for the first time in a long while, I actually had fun. I had no idea, as I danced freely in a field to Billie Eilish, that less than two weeks later, I'd be lying in Mum's garden, feeling so overwhelmed with the loss of another close friend that I wanted to disappear off the face of the earth.

Tyla called me on the afternoon of Sunday 3 July 2022. I was in my bedroom, about to have a snooze after meditating in the garden. I lay on my bed to take the call, looking forward to a good natter with Tyla. I honestly thought she was going to hit me with some juicy gossip when she said, 'Oh my God, Georgia, have you heard what happened?' I didn't have time to respond before Tyla's next sentence hurtled into my ear: 'Jake drove off a cliff in Turkey yesterday. He broke his neck and died instantly.'

I sat up fast, my heart banging. 'What, d'you mean Jake McLean?'

'Yeah, Jake,' said Tyla. 'I'm so sorry, Georgia.' My whole body went into convulsions. I collapsed sideways, buried my face in a pillow and screamed continuously. Mum shot into the room, and she was saying something as she tried to turn me over and calm me down, but all I could do was scream hysterically into that pillow. There was nothing Mum could do or say to console me.

I screamed for hours, until my voice all but disappeared. When I finally lifted my head from the pillow, Star was there with Mum. They'd heard the tragic news too. Mum had called all my friends, frantic with worry. The three of us hugged on the bed. 'First Cenk and now Jake,' I sobbed. 'The two boys who've played such a big part in my life are gone.'

Tyla and her mum, Joanne, came over. Bella, her mum, Lisa, and Aunty Sharon also joined us and we all sat in the garden. They tried to stop me from drinking, but I carried on topping up my wine glass, determined to drink myself into oblivion, replaying 'Perfect' on my phone. And that's how I ended up, sprawled on the grass, staring at the stars, saying, 'I don't want to be here. I don't want to be on this earth anymore. I want to be up there in the sky. With the stars. With Cenk and Jake.'

I slipped into the deepest grief imaginable in the days following Jake's death. Mum and my girlfriends worked on a rota-like system, taking turns to sit with me day and night as I lay in bed in the same stained tracksuit I'd been wearing since Tyla had called, uninterested in everything. Delirious and incoherent. I don't even remember Bella taking me into the bathroom, where she undressed me and got me into the bath. I didn't even know what day it was.

It's difficult to describe the grief I felt after losing Jake. My emotions were chaotic and confusing. Because I'd been in a sexual relationship with him, I had constant flashbacks to our moments of passion and romance, remembering all the times he'd made me feel loved. This added an extra layer to my grief.

Guilt hit me hard, too. You see, Jake and I had been messaging each other frequently before his death. We'd talked about our old times together, our favourite memories. And in one of his messages, he'd written: *I've always loved you, Georgia, and I always will.* For weeks, we went deep into our history, and I was beginning to think that maybe Jake and I would rekindle our relationship again. Jake had even invited me out to Turkey. 'Just get on a plane, Georgia,' he said. 'I want to fly you out here. I want to see you.' I wanted to see Jake too, but I was afraid our meeting would end in heartache again. So, I thought, *I'll see if the universe gives me signs suggesting I should go,* and little things happened, like our Ed Sheeran song, 'Perfect', would suddenly play on the radio or television. Jake kept messaging me, writing: *Come to Turkey. I can book your flights now.*

I'd messaged him back: *Look, don't book the flights yet. I want you to know that I do want to come, but I'm scared that you're going to hurt me.* Our conversation turned into a bit of a laugh back and forth. I was on the cusp of going to Turkey but, in the end, I didn't go. Olivia Attwood, one of my best friends and another fellow *Love Island* contestant, invited me on a last-minute work trip to Ibiza, so I went there instead, thinking, *This opportunity is a sure sign I shouldn't meet Jake.* In Ibiza, I chatted extensively to Olivia about my feelings for Jake. I really opened up to her as I knew she would never judge me. She's always been a friend I can talk to about anything – and I really appreciated her advice back then.

But I did beat myself up over this in those early days after Jake died, repeatedly asking myself the same questions. *Would Jake still be alive if I had gone to Turkey? If I had gone, would the car accident have happened? Jake was always such a good driver … it's so hard to imagine that he'd drive off a cliff.* Over time, I learned to let go of these negative thoughts. They wouldn't bring Jake back.

I truly couldn't have got through those times of grief without Mum and my friends. Mum helped me to take one day at a time. 'You won't feel this way forever, Georgia. I promise you,' she'd say every morning. Mornings were difficult; I'd wake up and, for a split second, I'd forget that Jake and Cenk had died, then I'd remember and feel devastated again.

Losing Cenk and Jake, the two most important men in my life, within months of one another, was horrendous. But slowly, I began to accept my grief. I'll never stop missing Cenk or Jake – they're with me every day. I strongly believe that when we lose someone, their energy alchemises into something else. Energy is never destroyed, it's only converted. Who knows, maybe one day Jake and Cenk's energies will alchemise. Imagine? If their strengths – friendship, loyalty, fun and passion – were mixed into one massive ball of energy inside one human being … then that person could become my perfect partner. That would be everything I've ever wished for.

Coping with grief is a waiting game; it's all about time, and blocking your emotions is detrimental in the long run. I know there'll be many readers who've gone through – or are going through – the pain of losing a loved one, and while I'm not a professional counsellor, I know from experience that when we acknowledge our emotions, they can

motivate us. Some days during my grief journey, I'd be rid-
dled with guilt if I'd forgotten about Cenk or Jake during
moments of joy. Now I know it's okay to have good days,
and when they happen, I think, *Yes, I'm going to get out there,
be resilient and make the most of my life, knowing that Cenk
and Jake are right beside me, smiling proudly.*

'YOU ARE WHATEVER
YOU CHOOSE TO
BELIEVE YOU ARE.'

'YOU HAVE
SOMETHING INSIDE
OF YOU THAT'S
STRONGER THAN
ANYTHING IN YOUR
OUTER WORLD.
CONNECT WITH IT, LET
IT BE YOUR SPIRITUAL
GUIDE – YOUR
COMPASS OF LIGHT
IN THE DARKNESS.'

Chapter Eight

TAKING BACK
MY SPIRITUALITY

As a kid, I was always interested in the spiritual world. I'd wonder, *Do we only go to heaven or hell – or is there another place?* and *How can fortune tellers predict your future?* I'd picture a veiled woman, ensconced in a dark caravan, gazing into a crystal ball with slithers of bright light dancing around it, seeing things that others can't see. The magic of it all fascinated me.

However, it wasn't until I turned seventeen, when my friend Tyla gifted me a copy of Rhonda Byrne's *The Secret*, that my eyes were opened to the fact that we can manifest our thoughts and control what happens in our lives rather than just letting life happen to us.

I was in a bad place when Tyla gave me *The Secret*. It was just after I'd split from Shane, my abusive ex-boyfriend. I didn't want to go out or do much. I'd go to Tyla and

Star's house – because there's such a lovely energy in their family – collapse on their sofa and cry my eyes out. I wasn't living to my full potential and Tyla noticed this. She was so excited when she handed me *The Secret*. She'd sensed my negative mindset and knew the book would help me. 'Honestly, Georgia, just give this a go. Seriously, it's wicked. It will help you to figure out your path in life. Trust me, it works,' she'd gushed.

Well, Tyla was right. She flicked a switch inside my head the second she introduced me to *The Secret*. I read it cover to cover, then re-read it, enthralled by its hopeful energy. No joke, it literally transformed my entire world.

I began to believe in a higher power – and that if you tap into that force, you can receive signs and synchronicities from the universe.

As I mentioned in chapter one, *The Secret*, which teaches you how to manifest your thoughts and dreams using the laws of attraction to change your life path, completely changed my outlook on the universe. I noticed people responding to me differently. They were more giving, more positive, more thankful. And the second I also decided to change the ways in which I view myself and world, and I saw the impact it had, I wanted to flick the same button that Tyla had switched for me in other people's minds.

I still write my manifestations today, following Byrne's three-step process to 'manifest your desires': I 'ask' for what I want to achieve, 'believe' in my dreams, and then visualise and appreciate 'receiving' these desires. Trust me, all my manifestations have come true – but only by adhering to these three steps.

After devouring *The Secret*, I couldn't wait to read *The Magic*, also written by Byrne. This book intrigued me as it's about the power of gratitude, as revealed in a two-thousand-year-old sacred text. Byrne takes you on a twenty-eight-day journey that ends with her teaching you how to apply the knowledge she shares to your life.

Many of my friends and relatives had completed the twenty-eight-day *Magic* journey. They raved about it and said it was life-changing, just like *The Secret*. So, I got stuck in and loved it, as I knew I would.

I started my *Magic* journey directly after reading *The Secret*, so I must still have been seventeen, possibly eighteen. But anyway, I remember I was temping – or trying to temp – at the time. Every weekday I'd catch the train to London Liverpool Street station, then walk around the corner to one of the agencies I'd signed with. I'd be there at 8 a.m., just before the agency opened, ready to start work. But often the bookers would say, 'Sorry, Georgia, we haven't got anything for you today.'

'Oh well,' I'd say, 'I guess I'll just sit here until you do have something for me.' Then I'd find a seat by the window at the front of the office and wait for a job to come in, reading *The Magic* while writing in my journal.

After a while, one of the bookers would stomp over and say something like, 'You can sit there from 8 a.m. until 8 p.m. if you want, Georgia, but unless someone calls in sick, you're not going to get a job.'

I'd smile politely and say, 'That's fine, I'll stay until 8 p.m. then. Thank you.' And then I'd carry on writing. I've always been driven.

In *The Magic*, Byrne asks you to make a daily list, over twenty-eight days, of all the things you're grateful for in life. Here are a few thoughts from my journal at that time:

1 – I'm truly grateful for having such a wonderful mum and the love she gave me this morning when she made breakfast for me.

2 – I'm truly blessed to have such amazing, beautiful and caring best friends – because they make my life worth living.

3 – I am so eternally grateful for my sense of humour – because it helps me connect with people.

4 – I am so happy and grateful for the band on my wrist as it brings me luck and connects me to God.

5 – I am so happy and grateful for my hair – because it is curly, thick and beautiful.

6 – Thank you, Mum, for always being there for me.

7 – Thank you, Bella, for all the fun and amazing times we've had that only you will experience with me.

8 – Thank you, Bella, for making me laugh until it hurts.

And so I'd go on, filling pages upon pages of everything I was thankful for, which was a lot. This filled me with such happiness. I began to look at the world with a new perspective. It's easy to bemoan what we don't have in life – that car or house or boyfriend, or more money, but by celebrating our 'haves', I found that you attract more opportunities and people into your life. Gratitude also helps you to see the best in other people, too.

At one point during the twenty-eight-day process, Byrne asks you to manifest a free cup of coffee – and to visualise somebody handing that cup of coffee to you. I did this. I pictured somebody – a kind-faced person – handing me a cup and saying, 'There you go, this one's on me.' Anyway, one morning I arrived at Liverpool Street extra early, around 7.30 a.m., eager as ever, and found myself at a loose end. The agency wasn't open yet, and I didn't want to hang about with all the suited commuters clogging the concourse of the station, zipping this way and that like manic beetles. So, I went for a stroll outside, towards Moorgate, and sat at an empty table outside a café. The sign on the café door read 'closed', so I figured nobody would mind me sitting there, at least until the gaff opened. This was the perfect opportunity for me to crack on with my gratitude list for the day, I thought.

I began writing, *I'm so grateful for the sunshine today. Thank you, Tyla and Star for helping me to believe in myself.* A shadow suddenly fell on the pages of my journal as a figure appeared beside me, radiating the sharp, nutty aroma of freshly brewed coffee. When I looked up, I met the cheery gaze of a man, probably aged around forty, in a white apron, clasping a takeaway cup, the door to the café visibly open over his shoulder. 'I hope I'm not disturbing you,' he said. 'Look, we're not open yet, but I thought you might like a coffee.' He put the steaming takeaway cup on the table beside my open journal. 'It's an Americano, with milk – is that okay? Would you like sugar?'

I gave him a big smile, reached for the cup then lifted it to indicate, *Cheers*. 'Thank you so much. This is perfect as it is. Obviously, I'll pay for it.' I put down the cup to forage in my bag, looking for my purse.

'No, no. This one's on the house,' said the man, palms raised in protest. 'As I said, we're not open yet, anyway. Please, enjoy your coffee.' Then he cocked his head towards the café. 'I'd better get back to work before opening time. You have a beautiful day though.'

I said, 'Oh my God, thank you. Thank you. I'm so grateful. You have a beautiful day, too.' I'm not kidding; God's truth, this happened. I walked away from the café, sipping my lovely coffee, thinking, *This is the first time in my life that somebody's given me a free cup of coffee, and I'd visualised this moment.* The bookers had nothing for me again that day, but I sat by the window again, opened my journal, and wrote: *Thank you to the lovely man who gave me a free cup of coffee this morning. I feel truly blessed by your kindness.*

Oh, I could bang on forever about Byrne's *The Secret* series, and I probably will – because, quite frankly, Byrne deserves a good big-up in these pages. Her books have shaped every aspect of my life, from my personal relation-ships to my career and mental wellbeing – and I'll never take that for granted.

*

Gratitude is everything in life – and *The Magic* galvanised this in my mind. I strongly believe in giving thanks to the universe for everything that makes us happy or stronger. Yes, we can be thankful for that new job, relationship, car or house or whatever, but we should also be grateful to the universe for getting us through shittier moments in life too.

I also believe that everything we do for people comes back to us. So, if people are cruel to others, then they'll 100 per cent get their comeuppance. I've also noticed how those who aren't helpful to others don't enjoy much luck in life.

But, you know, the smallest of kind gestures can change a person's entire day. I'm mindful of this; whenever somebody serves me in a shop, I'll look them in the eye and say thank you. I'll always be kind and helpful to others and, in return, when they thank me, I feel on top of the world. It's karma, isn't it? Little things mean a great deal to people.

When it comes to success, the universe can give you so much, provided you don't get above yourself. If you get carried away, believing that you are better than others, your ego will take over your spirit – then the universe has a clever way of putting you on your arse. So, it's important to know that you're not above, or below, anybody else.

As children, we're often told, 'You can be anything you want to be,' but this is also true for adults. If you believe in yourself, and really visualise your dreams, it's possible to achieve them. Honestly, I don't think it matters how old you are. I'm constantly reading inspirational stories online about people who've started their dream business in their forties, fifties or even later. For instance, I read a story recently about a woman in her late-forties who launched a fashion brand that really took off.

I love reading about how famous people got their breaks, at all ages. Look at Oprah Winfrey: she started out as a twenty-something news anchor at Baltimore's WJZ-TV, but the network fired her for being 'too emotional' when reporting devastating stories. Credit to Oprah; her empathy helped her to turn things around and create one of the most popular talk shows ever, aged thirty-two.

Tony Robbins's career path is incredible; he was a broke janitor before he became a premier 'performance coach' in his mid-twenties, filling stadiums with his inspirational talks. He's now the biggest face in his sector, full stop. Tony also champions gratitude, which has undoubtedly played a major role in his success. I agree wholeheartedly when Tony says: 'When you are grateful, fear disappears, and abundance appears.' This is so true, and I reiterate: we get back what we give.

After devouring Byrne's *The Secret* series, I became addicted to self-help and spiritual books. Every available space in my bedroom is now crammed with them. I'd be totally lost without these books.

Power vs Force and *The Map of Consciousness Explained: A Proven Energy Scale to Actualize Your Ultimate Potential*, both by Dr David R. Hawkins, are among my go-to books. Hawkins says consciousness is the 'ability to experience and understand yourself and your environment', and that your mind has access to a universal consciousness shared by all people. His *Map of Consciousness* is based on his muscle-testing calibration experiments, which define emotions and values corresponding to levels of consciousness. These emotions include shame, guilt, apathy, fear, reason, courage, pride, anger, acceptance, love and the 'higher' energies of peace, ecstasy and enlightenment.

Hawkins's *Map of Consciousness* helps you to become a happier person by understanding why you feel certain emotions – this is my take on it anyway.

Mostly, I learned a lot about authenticity in *Power vs Force*. One calibration experiment was based on two people looking at the same image in two formats: an original painting and a replica of the painting. This made me think about how we portray ourselves, especially on social media. Even if you don't look or feel perfect, your authentic self is far better than a pretend version of you.

According to Hawkins's experiments, pride vibrates at a lower level than acceptance. I reflected on this in relation to how many of us fret about our looks. Compared to how I once viewed myself – back in the day when Shane branded me 'disgusting', for example – I now try to accept my appearance, and I'm a happier person for it. We shouldn't obsess about what others might be thinking about us – because most of the time, those people are worrying about you judging *them*.

Changing your inner beliefs holds the key to transforming your reality to a higher level in which the universe responds better to you. For many of us, our insecurities stem from challenging childhood experiences. Healers say we should go back to our childhoods to understand these insecurities and reframe them in our minds. Recently, my spiritual guide, Rob, introduced me to past-life meditation, a practice in which you revisit your childhood in your mind then try to reframe early moments of insecurity. Through meditation, the aim is to rewrite your childhood by acknowledging those fears and giving love and gratitude to your younger self. Here's a hypothetical example: you were just a little girl, sitting quietly in the classroom when a boy suddenly yanked your hair, spat in your face and sneered, 'You're an ugly pig'. You went home and cried all night, feeling hurt, abused and ashamed. You thought, *I'm an ugly pig. Why was that boy horrible to me? Is it because I'm different to the other girls?* You then carried those cruel words with you into adulthood. Via past-life meditation, you'd go back to that little girl and give her love and comfort. You'd say to her, 'You were a good, loving girl. You were just an innocent girl who didn't deserve to be hurt.'

During my past-life meditation, I journeyed back to my twelve-year-old self. I pictured myself lying in bed, crying my eyes out after being bullied by schoolkids over my psoriasis. I gave myself love and told myself, *It was the bullies who had issues, not you.* I came away from that session feeling peaceful and confident in my head.

Social media can really harm your self-confidence if you're not careful. I think we've all compared ourselves to others at some point, haven't we? What you see, however, isn't always reality: a friend may post a picture depicting her perfect family set-up – the gorgeous husband, their perfect toddler and newborn baby, and you'll sit there thinking, *I wish I had her life*. But for all you know, she could be having a shitty day as you're looking at her Facebook page: she's had a row with the gorgeous husband, the baby's been sick over her, the toddler's got her in a headlock ... You know what I'm saying: don't compare yourself to others. It drains your energy and diminishes your aura. I suggest watching spiritual talks on YouTube instead – or meditating, which plays a huge part in my life.

There are two methods that I rely on. There's deep meditation, which I practice during yoga sessions, when I silence my mind but acknowledge the energies in my body. Yoga is so important for slowing down; it allows you to identify your inner tensions, then release them through deep breathing. The other type of meditation is what I call 'meditation for myself', which is basically when I take time out for me. I'll go for a walk in the forest, read a book, get my nails done or go for a coffee. Any activity that gives me headspace. It's all about being present in the moment. This is so important. Even dedicating ten minutes to yourself a day is so effective for rejuvenating your mind and soul. Many people think meditation is a waste of time. It's not; it's as valuable as going for a run or going to the office. Meditation, in any form, is about slowing down and making the most of life.

Spirituality has massively helped me through some of the toughest points in my life, and I did experience a spiritual awakening during my Bear sex-tape ordeal. Even at times when my faith was slightly shattered, I knew deep down that everything would work out for me and that Bear would get his karma, as my dear friend Cenk had predicted. Subconsciously, I recognised, *This is the stage of your life when things are meant to fall apart.* But, at the end of the day, my faith did get me through that testing period – I knew the universe had my back. Whenever I felt numb and helpless, I'd receive little signs and synchronicities – a butterfly would fly in through the window; I'd see Cenk's number on the oven clock display or on the television. I'd hear Cenk or Jake's voices in my head, telling me they loved me and that everything will be fine. And I could almost hear the universe communicating with me, saying, 'Look, I'm here. You're right on track. Stay strong.'

My faith in the universe today is stronger than ever. I mean, it's got me through some difficult shit, right? Every day, I manifest and write my gratitude lists. Nothing means more to me than my beautiful friends and family – and they're always at the top of my gratitude lists. As far as my manifestations go, I do ask for love. I visualise being in a happy relationship, but I acknowledge this will only happen when the timing is right. Say the universe had given me the husband, children and white picket fence ten years ago? I'd be pottering about in the kitchen now, getting the kids' tea on. I would be consumed with that existence – I certainly wouldn't be writing this book – and I might've missed my purpose in life, which, I believe, is to help and inspire people. So, I'll let the universe do its thing – if it ain't broken, as they say ... And finally, some words of encouragement to you, my lovely readers: be grateful, be kind to one another, be present, have faith in yourself and the universe. Be the best version of yourself – because nobody is as special as you.

'WORRYING IS JUST WISHING FOR SOMETHING YOU DON'T WANT TO HAPPEN. NO AMOUNT OF ANXIETY WILL CHANGE THE OUTCOME OF FUTURE EVENTS. SO STAY PRESENT AND STAY POSITIVE.'

'WE ARE ALL
CONNECTED. THE
MORE LOVE AND
COMPASSION WE
GIVE ONE ANOTHER,
THE MORE IS
RETURNED TO US.'

Chapter Nine

TAKING BACK
MY POWER

Even before Stephen Bear was convicted, I'd receive a constant stream of messages from people urging me to create accounts on internet subscription channels. *With your profile, you should get on OnlyFans,* messages in my social-media inboxes suggested. Other followers sent me statistics stating how much I could expect to earn by posting videos and pictures of myself on these channels, their views inspired by images they'd seen on my Instagram page – shots of me in a bikini, for example. *Some people make £100,000 a month doing this kind of stuff,* I was told.

Now, I won't lie, it was extremely tempting to think, *I could make over a million pounds a year – just by twerking or jumping some rope in my underwear.* But seeing how sexually explicit the content is on some platforms, I decided not to go down that road. I wanted a career in television, not the porn industry. This is my body, my choice, right? Yet still, a video of me engaged in private sexual acts ended up on every popular porn site in the UK – because Bear posted and sold this footage online without my consent.

I never judge those who choose to be on platforms like OnlyFans or PornHub. I think people should do whatever makes them happy; some women and men enjoy being sexy and making a load of money in the process – and why shouldn't they? But these people should be protected. Nobody else should *ever* distribute their content without consent.

After being exploited on porn sites, I was shocked to learn how so many of these platforms are profiting from non-consensual videos and, in some cases, even child pornography. What scared me most, however, was the sheer number of image-based sexual abuse victims who reached out to me during and after Bear's trial. I'm so fortunate that Bear was convicted, but many of the women who contacted me said they couldn't even get the perpetrators of the crimes against them arrested, let alone seek justice. And several other victims whose perpetrators did face revenge porn charges lost their cases after the court ruled 'intent to cause distress' had not been proven. I couldn't get my head around this; these women opened up to me, saying sexually explicit images or footage of them had been posted on social-media and porn sites without their knowledge, and those images still remained online for all to see. Reading their messages, it was blatant to me the resulting trauma these women were going through. Like me, they said they felt violated, humiliated, used and utterly devastated. It hurt me to think that other revenge porn victims hadn't got justice because they couldn't 'prove' their suffering in court. I thought, *They shouldn't have to prove their distress. Their perpetrators should be prosecuted. End of.*

Looking at figures obtained under the Freedom of Information Act by domestic abuse charity Refuge, I was staggered at how few charges are made in reported revenge porn cases. According to the statistics, 13,860 'intimate image' offences were recorded across twenty-four UK police forces between 1 January 2019 and 31 July 2022, but only 4 per cent of those alleged offenders were charged or summonsed. Twenty-two per cent of the recorded offences resulted in no further action due to 'evidential difficulties'.

Revenge porn was criminalised in 2015, but the government's Online Safety Bill, when it came into force in March 2022, stated that prosecutors had to prove an intention to cause 'humiliation or distress'. The bill aims 'to ensure social media companies respond to and prevent online violence' against women and girls. It was clear to me that this 'intention' loophole regarding revenge porn meant some victims didn't have a leg to stand on when taking legal action. And with the rise of subscription platforms giving individuals opportunities to run porn sites, causing 'distress' no longer seemed the sole motivator for breaking this law. Some perpetrators say they didn't mean to cause distress, claiming they only posted non-consensual footage for monetary gain, or to 'show off'. I wanted to do something about this. I mean, I'm no politician, but the solution seemed a no-brainer to me: if the government were to change the Online Safety Bill by taking out the 'intent to cause distress' clause, then thousands of other revenge porn victims could win justice.

People sometimes ask me, 'Do you think your case would have got as much attention if you and Bear weren't in the public eye?' This is a valid question. Without my or Bear's reality-television backgrounds, I don't think the media would have gone as big on my story as they did. But I'm glad they pulled out the big guns – because it gave me a voice and platform to speak to the younger generation and launch my campaign to change the Online Safety Bill, which I started immediately after Bear was sentenced to twenty-one months in jail – and I've never looked back.

On the morning of 20 March 2023, I went on *GMB* to chat with former Labour politician and broadcaster Ed Balls and his co-host, Susanna Reid, about my ITV documentary which was due to air that evening. Already, ITV was broadcasting a teaser for *Revenge Porn: Georgia vs Bear*, featuring a clip of me reading my statement to the press on the court steps following Bear's sentencing; it was overlaid with text reading: *Georgia had sex with an ex. He filmed it. She asked him to delete. He didn't. He shared. She went to the police. He was found guilty and sentenced to twenty-one months in prison. This is her story.*

Indeed, this was my story in a nutshell: my trauma, my struggle in the face of shame, my grief, my justice, my voice, and hopefully now, my power – to fight for other women and make a difference. Bring it on.

I used my opportunity on the *GMB* sofa to speak about the pain Bear had inflicted upon me to illustrate the need for legal reform. I told Ed and Susanna how I'd felt extremely exploited and hurt in what had been a 'devastating time for me'. I then explained that one of the biggest hurdles in revenge porn cases was the requirement for victims to prove 'intent to cause distress'. My hosts nodded encouragingly when I said, 'So it's to prove that someone knew you'd be distressed if they shared these explicit videos or pictures, but I just think it's common sense: obviously if someone does share that, it is a [cause of] distress. What I really want other victims to know is: don't feel like you can't come forward. The only thing that's shameful is distribution without consent.'

Ed then asked me if I'd ever considered stepping into politics. This gave me a proper lift; nobody had ever asked me that question before. If he'd suggested this to me about two-and-a-half years ago, I would've laughed and said, 'Shut up, I don't know the first thing about politics.' That morning, I straightened my back, looked my hosts straight in the eye, and said, 'Over the past two years I've spoken to victims on a daily basis. I've really educated myself on this, so I feel I have the skills to take this forward.'

During the ad break, Ed praised my campaign and agreed that the flaw in the Online Safety Bill must be addressed. 'I'll put you in touch with the right politicians,' he said. Wow, I couldn't thank him enough. This was a huge step in the right direction. I left the ITV studios feeling all kick-ass and happy, but also slightly overwhelmed, wondering, *Can I really speak with politicians? Will they change the law? For me? For other victims? Bloody hell, imagine if they do?*

What a day. First, I called for a law change, then my documentary went out to the British public. Watching it with Mum ignited within me all the emotions I'd encountered since December 2020, when the guy from *The Challenge* Tea Page had sent me that screenshot capturing me having sex with Bear in his garden – footage that Bear had already uploaded on OnlyFans. One Instagram video in *Revenge Porn: Georgia vs Bear* sees me in my hotel bathroom in Dubai – where I was working as an influencer for the winter season – about an hour before I received that screenshot of the footage. In this clip, I'm wearing a cropped T-shirt and bikini bottoms while filming myself on a digital camcorder. I tell my followers I'm getting ready to go to the beach club (which I was doing at that point). 'I'm just feeling so extremely grateful right now,' I say. Then you see me swigging from a champagne bottle, my nails painted a hopeful coral as I narrate retrospectively, 'Here I was, in Dubai, living my best life. What I didn't realise, though, is that I'd just flown into my worst nightmare.'

In the next video I recorded that day, which I sent to my friends Nicole Charbass, Olivia Attwood, Clelia Theodorou and Francesca Parman, and featured in my documentary, I'm sobbing my eyes out, face smudged with mascara, hair like tumbleweed, saying, 'What am I gonna do, girls? I can't carry this on. I'm sorry to send you a message tonight. I know it's weird because I'm just in on my own.' Seeing those two recordings again reminded me of how I went from the happy-go-lucky, hopeful and grateful me to a girl so ashamed and grief-stricken that she couldn't leave her hotel room. I remembered the evening two weeks after I'd seen the damning screenshot, when I'd woken, shaking with chills but sweating buckets. Just as I recalled coming round in a Dubai hospital bed, attached to a drip with a doctor standing over me, saying my body had gone into septic shock due to a burst ovarian cyst. I heard his words in my head again: 'You're very lucky, Miss Harrison. If you'd left it another twenty-four hours, you might not have made it.' And I said to Mum, as we sat thigh to thigh on the sofa, 'I nearly died. How did we get through all of that?'

Mum squeezed my hand in hers. 'We got through it because we're strong, sweetie,' she said. 'Because *you're* strong.' Then Mum appeared on the television screen, recalling how she'd dealt with the hundreds of emails that deluged her inbox after my sex video went viral.

'Well,' I said, 'I couldn't have done this without you. Thank you ... for always being there for me. You're a fucking star.'

Mum laughed. 'Right back at you, Georgia.'

Though it recorded some of my darkest moments, I was thrilled with the documentary, which completely encapsulated my initial vision for the film: to show that I'm an everyday girl who'd been put through the mill; to be my authentic self after being hushed for so long while Bear

197

had ridiculed and tried to discredit my side of the story with overt lies. The response from the public to *Revenge Porn: Georgia vs Bear* was humbling and uplifting at once. Of course, a few trolls ranted on my Instagram link to the documentary, moaning that I should've known better than to get with a man like Bear – like I was supposed to have *guessed* he'd film us having intercourse. I ignored those comments and instead loved all the heartfelt, encouraging ones from those who'd applauded my 'bravery'. People also commented on my *GMB* interview, backing my campaign to shake up the Online Safety Bill to protect existing and future victims. My side of the story out there, I could now venture into the corridors of power and give it some serious welly ... couldn't I?

True to his word, Ed Balls hooked me up with the Right Honourable Caroline Nokes, Conservative MP and chairwoman of the Women and Equalities Committee. I was beyond grateful for this introduction.

Later that week, I headed to the Houses of Parliament to meet Caroline, armed with some printed messages from the revenge porn victims who'd contacted me. Blimey, I'd expected to walk straight into the Palace of Westminster, but I had to join a massive security queue that snaked around the corner. Standing in that stationary queue, my nerves began to kick in. *Would I be able to pull this off? Am I going to be late because I'm stuck in this queue?* Then, just as I replaced those negative thoughts with, *Ah, the universe will tell you what to say,* a pretty woman with gorgeous swishy brunette hair and a sharp smile approached me, proffering her hand. 'Hi, Georgia, I'm Caroline. Lovely to meet you. Now, quick, quick, let's get you to the front of this queue.'

I thought, *Wow, she's so glamorous!* Caroline fast-tracked us through security, then we sat down in the main coffee area, where suited MPs clustered around tables, engaged in intense conversations. Caroline put me at ease from the get-go. 'You're an incredibly brave young woman, Georgia,' she said, reading my case studies. 'This is a huge and incredibly important campaign that sends out the message that online abuse against women and girls cannot go on.'

'Thank you, Caroline,' I said, glimpsing the important people in the room over my coffee cup. It felt surreal, but in a nice way. 'I just think it's a simple thing. If we can remove the "intent to cause distress" clause from the Online Safety Bill, then hopefully other victims of this evil crime can also get guilty verdicts for their perpetrators. And let's face it, *any* person who finds unconsented footage of themselves, on *any* online platform, is going to feel distressed. Violated, actually.'

Caroline nodded, a serious political expression on her face now. 'I'm going to do everything in my power to help you, Georgia,' she said. 'I can put you in touch with the right people. But I must say, don't hold your breath. It does usually take a long time to get stuff like this over the line. Things don't happen overnight in politics; people will tell you they'll get things done for you, but it's not that simple when it comes to changing the law.'

'Yeah, I know. I really appreciate everything you're doing for me, Caroline. Honestly, I didn't expect to get this far.'

The following Wednesday, Caroline mentioned my campaign during Prime Minister's Questions in the House of Commons. I watched this on television, in awe of Caroline's energy and firm composure as she asked the then-Deputy Prime Minister Dominic Raab to review my calls to change the Online Safety Bill. She said, 'Georgia Harrison is an incredibly brave young woman who only got justice when she was a victim of revenge porn because she could prove that the perpetrator intended to cause her distress.

'Most victims cannot prove that, and perpetrators are using platforms to use revenge porn for financial gain. That is not covered in the legislation. Will my right honourable friend commit to looking at the case studies Georgia has compiled and to reviewing the legislation to strengthen it and make it more effective?'

A chorus of 'hear, hear' rose from the green-leather benches. 'Hear, Hear,' I said. Fucking right, I did. This was huge.

Dominic stood up next. He confirmed changes to the Online Safety Bill would be 'considered', including the 'creation of a new base offence of sharing intimate images without consent that don't require proof of any intent to cause distress'. This was great news, but I remained mindful of Caroline's heads-up about laws not changing overnight.

Things really took off from there. My schedule was chock-a-block with radio and television interviews as I spread my message wide. Meanwhile, more victims who hadn't secured convictions messaged me on the back of my documentary and interviews. Understandably, they felt cheated. *How come you got justice, but I didn't?* they'd ask. My God, I felt so sad reading these messages. Most of the victims' cases had collapsed in court – because they couldn't prove 'intent to cause distress'. I would have been heartbroken if my case had gone that way.

I continued working with charities, including Not Your Porn and South West Grid for Learning (SWGfL)'s Revenge Porn Helpline, and supporting Refuge's campaign against revenge porn, alongside Zara McDermott, another former *Love Island* contestant who was twice subjected to intimate-image abuse. Zara, who also filmed a documentary on revenge porn, sent me a lovely message expressing her 'love and support' after I posted my Instagram plea for information when the garden footage went viral. Kate Isaacs, founder of Not Your Porn, said media interest in her campaign to make hosting non-consensual content illegal had gathered momentum since Zara and I had gone public with our stories.

Towards the end of April 2023, prior to taking a much-needed break at Jason Vale's Juice Master Retreat in Portugal, I got an email from Labour Party leader Sir Keir Starmer's office, inviting me to speak at a round-table event about tackling violence against women and girls (VAWG) in two days' time. I'd read about Sir Keir's mission to halve

VAWG ahead of the next election, so I hoped the meeting would keep the Tory government on its toes about the issue. I'd be able to voice my campaign at the round table, so there was no way I was going to miss it, even though it'd mean missing the first two days of my juice retreat and shelling out to change my flight out there.

Getting to the event was stressful; I had to lug my heavy suitcase as I was heading to Portugal straight from the meeting, and I felt weary after my first two days of the juice diet, which I'd started at home in Essex. But it was well worth the effort to take part in this important discussion. I joined other campaigners, including actress Emily Atack, around the table with Sir Keir and Shadow Home Secretary Yvette Cooper at St Giles Trust, the charity hosting the event, in Camberwell, south London. I also met Jess Phillips, an advocate for tackling VAWG and a fabulous character in the world of politics.

Sir Keir asked me to kick off the discussion. I felt quite overwhelmed. My stomach growled as I spoke, but I was determined to make the most of this opportunity. Once I started, however, my words came easily. I introduced myself, then launched right into it. 'So many women have been let down by the justice system,' I said. 'There are loopholes that allow perpetrators to avoid conviction in cases of image-based sexual abuse. Social media and online platforms must be held accountable for what they are allowing to happen on their sites to get more users.'

The meeting was empowering. Emily, who had fronted a documentary about cyber-flashing, said she'd suffered sexual harassment from the age of ten. She gave an impassioned speech, saying, 'I've experienced extreme levels of sexual harassment, abuse and sexual assault.

'This was something that I just had to put up with, but it was also behaviour that I realised that I was kind of brainwashed into thinking was my fault.

'I feel that I'm at a point in my life now where I'm very tired of apologising for who I am. I'm sick of feeling guilty for simply just existing.'

This resonated with me; for so long, I blamed myself for having sex with Bear, thinking, *It's my fault. I should never have gone to his house that day.* I remembered only too well the days I spent locked inside my hotel room in Dubai, too ashamed to show my face to the world, grieving my former self. Feeling stripped of my dignity, my innocent spark gone for good with one click of an upload button. But it wasn't my fault – I knew this now – and at least my experience had brought me here today to enforce the message: violence against women and girls is *not* normal, it is *not* acceptable, and the government must change laws to make this country safer for women and girls.

Our round-table chat generated headlines, including: *Actress Emily Atack and* Love Island *star Georgia Harrison speak at discussion with Keir Starmer about tackling violence against women and girls.* I was so glad I made the effort to go to that meeting; I wanted as much press coverage as possible for my campaign, and I knew the impact would be huge.

Around this time, Bear was also getting a fair amount of media attention as he served his sentence in Chelmsford

Prison. One story told how Bear was a 'broken man on suicide watch' because he 'didn't expect to be jailed' for his crime. A 'prison insider' told the *Sun*: 'He's at his lowest ebb. He's been crying for days.' Other papers said Bear was earning £3.60 packing tea and coffee for fellow inmates in the nick. His fiancée was still standing by her man, posting on TikTok a video she filmed inside the visitors' waiting room at HMP Chelmsford. In another TikTok clip, she claimed she'd applied for a prison cleaning job so she could be 'closer' to Bear. Honestly, those two are made for each other.

I didn't pay much attention to those Bear jail stories – my 'prison source' told me, 'He's very quiet in here'. Besides, I had my own stuff to get on with – and the universe was aligning in my favour.

On top of running my campaign to abolish the 'intent to cause distress' clause, I was also rebuilding my career. Many brands wouldn't go near me as an influencer after my sex-tape scandal broke, which left me struggling financially. I do love it, though, when someone offers you an olive branch, and one company gave me that opportunity in February 2021, just after Bear's arrest – even though I wasn't hot property then.

WooWoo, a firm that sells intimate female products, signed me for a year as their global ambassador. I'll admit, I was a bit nervous about this as WooWoo sells lube, and I didn't feel comfortable promoting sexual products amid the garden-tape fiasco. But the people at WooWoo respected my integrity and let me promote their other products such as hair-removal creams and feminine washes. They were amazing – the brand pretty much got me through that difficult year. I didn't realise just how much WooWoo did for me as a brand until after the court case – they gave me the olive branch of all olive branches and I'll always be so thankful for this.

In mid-June 2023, Superdrug signed me to front their 'You Before Yes' campaign which is right up my street as its aim is to 'tackle destructive non-consensual sexual behaviours'.

As part of the campaign, Superdrug is launching its own brand of condoms, complete with a reminder about the importance of consent on the packaging. I'm so proud to be the face of 'You Before Yes'; the campaign is a great step forwards in educating and empowering young people to find their voices and stay safe. To demonstrate the importance of respectful, consensual sexual behaviour, Superdrug filmed me reading out some of the horrific, sexually explicit DMs I've received from strangers. I won't share these disgusting messages here – you can hear them online if you wish – but I hope they inspire others to call out non-consensual behaviour.

As well as campaigning, influencing (brands are keen to hire me again nowadays) and penning this book, I've also recently landed my next television gig. As I write, I can't reveal details about this opportunity (sorry) as I'm sworn to secrecy, but let's just say, I know it will test my strength and resilience in unimaginable ways – and I'm super excited to be back in the telly game.

Talk about everything happening at once. I'd just finished filming my piece for 'You Before Yes' when Caroline Nokes contacted me again. 'I've got you a meeting with Lord Chancellor and Secretary of State for Justice, Alex Chalk KC, and Justice Minister Edward Argar at the Ministry of Justice on the morning of Monday 26 June,' she said.

This blew me away. *The Lord Chancellor wants to meet me?* But there was a problem. I was due to fly to the other side of the world to start filming on 24 June. I had to tell Caroline that I couldn't make that date, but then, as luck would have it, the universe did its best again. A couple of hours later, I got a call saying my filming had been pushed back slightly. I would now be flying on the evening of 26 June, which meant I could meet the Lord Chancellor after all. Happy days.

Caroline didn't go into specific details about my forthcoming meeting, but I presumed it would be another chance to chat about my idea to change the Online Safety Bill. I didn't expect the Lord Chancellor to turn around and say, 'Okay then, Georgia, I've looked into your request, and I think it's a goer. I'll change the Online Safety Bill for you. Job done.' Do you know what I mean? But I thought maybe he'd say he was considering removing the intent flaw. Either way, I wasn't anticipating a definitive answer because, as Caroline had told me, 'It does usually take a long time to get stuff like this over the line.'

On the day before my meeting with the Lord Chancellor, I was busy doing some promotional work for the vodka brand Silq, with Mum and Bella. I put on a pink playsuit, to match the strawberry vodka, and we got the camera rolling, knocking back a few glasses of Silq as we did so, obviously. I did a voiceover for my video, reciting one of my favourite quotes from the late 'philosophical entertainer' Alan Watts: 'The meaning of life is just to be alive. It is so plain and so obvious and so simple. And yet, everybody rushes around in a great panic as if it were necessary to achieve something beyond themselves. This is the real secret to life: to be completely engaged with what you are doing in the here and now.' I finished by relating this quote to the product, adding, 'That's one of my favourite quotes by Alan Watts, and I wanted to remind you that, sometimes, it's okay to let loose and have a bit of fun with the people you love ... especially when Silq rose vodka's involved.'

We were fully embracing this 'fun' vibe. Once I'd filmed my promo, Mum, Bella and I had a couple more Silqs; they were going down a treat on that boiling Sunday afternoon. Well, around 5 p.m., as the three of us larked about in Mum's kitchen, I picked up my phone to check my messages and, when I scrolled through my emails, I saw one from the Ministry of Justice, sent to me two days previously. I was like, *Fuck, how the hell did I miss that?* When I opened the email, I almost fell over. I thought maybe I was having a Silq-induced hallucination. There it was, in black and white, staring me in the face. The email stated, quite simply, that the Ministry of Justice had decided to make an amendment to the Online Safety Bill: to remove the 'intent to cause distress' clause. The

Lord Chancellor would confirm this at our meeting on Monday, apparently.

Mum piped up then, 'What is it, Georgia? What are you looking at?'

I looked up at Mum and Bella, on the brink of laughter, or tears? I wasn't sure, really, I was surprised more than anything. 'They're changing the law,' I said, handing my phone to Mum. 'Look, read the email. They're changing the Online Safety Bill. For me. For all the other victims.'

Bella laughed. 'You're joking, right?'

'Oh, sweetie, I'm so proud of you,' said Mum, crying.

We all sobered up fast – after a celebratory, jumping-up-and-down group hug and shouts of 'cheers', naturally. I can't begin to tell you how elated I felt in that moment. After all the shame and guilt and grief I'd suffered, I'd turned my trauma into something positive. Hopefully, now other victims of revenge porn will get the justice they deserve.

The next day, I proudly put on my suit and went to the Ministry of Justice. Before now, I'd spoken eloquently about my campaign – so people had told me, anyway. Today, I felt a bit tongue-tied as I stepped into the meeting room, where the Lord Chancellor and Justice Minister Edward Argar greeted me.

Alex Chalk KC looked younger than I'd expected: very smart and well put together, with immaculate dark hair and a friendly smile. My natural reaction was to hug him, but I didn't think this would be appropriate, so we shook hands and sat down to chat, TV cameras trained on us.

My voice wobbled slightly. 'Sorry, I feel a bit emotional,' I said to Alex Chalk. 'This is what I've been campaigning for, and I just want to say thank you for changing the law. This is going to make a huge difference to so many other women and men out there.'

Alex Chalk explained why he'd chosen to change the Online Safety Bill. He basically said, 'Look, the government utterly hears you and everything you've said. We've spent a lot of time going over image-based sexual abuse and the flaws in the Online Safety Bill, and we agree with everything you've been saying.'

'This has been a deeply personal campaign for me. I can't tell you how grateful I am,' I replied.

Alex Chalk spread his hands. 'Well, if there's ever anything you want to discuss regarding image-based sexual abuse or violence against women and girls, you can have those conversations with me. You're now a middle voice between victims and the government, Georgia.'

I didn't really want to throw anything else in there. I mean, this guy had just changed the law for me. But I couldn't help but point out how some victims' images often remain online, even after their perpetrators have been convicted. 'Are there any plans in place for these online platforms to be held accountable for unconsented material?' I asked.

'Absolutely,' said Alex Chalk. He then explained a new clause within the Online Safety Bill that states platforms could be fined up to 10 per cent of their annual earnings for not removing non-consensual pictures or footage. This was another unexpected bonus. I thanked Alex Chalk and Justice Minister Edward Argar again, then went outside to speak to a *GMB* reporter, bright sunshine beating down on my face, warming my soul. When I was asked how I felt about the change to the law, I said, 'It's still sinking in, everything that's happened today. It's been overwhelmingly emotional, and it felt like almost the end of my journey. In a good way, like I'd really achieved something. I feel so strong, so empowered, I feel so grateful to everyone who supported my campaign, to everyone who let me know I've got nothing to be ashamed of, and I just hope I can let other victims know, they have absolutely nothing to be ashamed of. The people who should be ashamed are those who break the law.'

I didn't get the chance to watch a replay of my interview that day. As usual, I was in a mad hurry. I left the Ministry of Justice, phone bleeping like crazy with tonnes of congratulatory messages, jumped in a taxi home, collected my suitcase and headed to London Heathrow Airport to catch my flight to the other side of the world. Well, the first of two flights, but that's as much as I can tell you about my next television project.

A few hours later, some 35,000 ft up in the sky, my mind was still awhirl with thoughts. *Did my campaigning really just change the law?* I looked out of the plane window at the frothy bed of clouds below me, a beautiful reminder of how lucky we are to be in this world and all that we can achieve. I pressed my forehead against the clear acrylic, closed my eyes and breathed in and out, in and out. *Yes,*

your campaigning changed the law. You fucking smashed it.
Then I turned around in my seat, ordered a glass of red
from the flight attendants who just happened to be passing
with the drinks trolley (thank you, universe), and sat back
and focused on enjoying that wine – because, as my good
mate Alan Watts, God rest his soul, once said, 'This is the
real secret to life: to be completely engaged with what you
are doing in the here and now.'

Yeah, smashed it.

'RECOVERING FROM
IMAGE-BASED
SEXUAL ABUSE IS A
GRIEVING PROCESS;
IT'S LIKE LOSING A
CLOSE FRIEND OR
FAMILY MEMBER.'

'YOU HAVE NOTHING TO BE ASHAMED OF; THE ONLY PERSON WHO SHOULD FEEL SHAME IS THE PERSON WHO POSTED THE PICTURES OR FOOTAGE ONLINE.'

Chapter Ten

TAKING BACK
YOUR POWER

The public response I received when I won my crusade to amend the Online Safety Bill was immense. Hundreds of people congratulated me, expressing their gratitude that hopefully, the revision would deter would-be perpetrators, encourage more victims to come forward, and help other image-based sexual abuse victims to win justice.

Many of my followers were shocked at the government's speedy response to my campaign to abolish the 'intent to cause distress' clause. 'I thought it took months, years even, to change the law,' wrote one follower. I thought the same, but I'm so unbelievably happy that Alex Chalk understood my concerns and acted so swiftly. This change in the law has definitely opened up a wider public conversation about image-based sexual abuse and the impact that this sickening crime has on people's mental health and on society in general. And we *need* these conversations. These are important discussions that might not have happened if my case hadn't been so public. Victims now know that they *are* entitled to justice.

Image-based sexual abuse is scarily prevalent in the UK but, fortunately, more people are now coming forward to speak about – and report – their experiences.

During the month of Bear's sentencing, March 2023, the Revenge Porn Helpline received 406 calls, compared with 260 in the previous month. Following the amendment to the Online Safety Bill on 27 June 2023, I spoke with the Revenge Porn Helpline manager, Sophie Mortimer, who asked me to include the statement below in this book. Her words brought tears to my eyes, while also echoing my views that, as technology progresses, further measures will be needed in the future to help combat the scourge of revenge porn.

Sophie said:

> The impact of the sharing of intimate images without consent is devastating, but it has been hard to see that widely recognised in the public eye. Georgia's incredible bravery, waiving her anonymity around the trial, and speaking openly about the consequences of the abuse she experienced, has been game changing. Her documentary showed the raw emotion she experienced and the reality of what it meant for her as well as her family.
>
> But as well as being open about the low points, Georgia has been able to use her experience and

what she has learnt to become an inspiring focal point for all those who have suffered similar experiences: she has given a voice to the voiceless. She has campaigned fearlessly, and her achievements in bringing the truth of her experience to the public consciousness should not be underestimated.

We will all benefit from her work, growing the understanding of what the impact of intimate image abuse is really like for those who experience it.

I think it's inevitable that there will be more work to do on this. These forms of abuse are changing all the time as technology develops with new tools, new platforms, and new ways of interacting online. It will take time for the impact of the changed legislation to be felt, and I have no doubt that in five years or so, we will again be campaigning for change. That's the nature of the internet, and the nature of people: change. Those of us working in this area know that we're in it for the long haul.

I couldn't agree more – and I know that I'm in this for the long haul.

More alleged victims reached out to me, too. Women who'd fought their cases but didn't get a conviction thanked me for taking the matter forward, adding that they were relieved that other victims will hopefully not endure the same disappointment. But it's not just women who fall prey to image-based sexual abuse.

Amid the media coverage surrounding my case and legal campaign, a man, whom I won't name, wrote to me about his alleged 'revenge porn' ordeal and the huge impact it has had on his life and career.

His message devastated me; I felt his anguish in every sentence. He told me he'd had sex in a hotel with two women he met on a night out in London. 'It was supposed to be a bit of fun, a laugh,' he wrote, 'we all consented – and the women filmed our threesome. We agreed to keep this private moment to ourselves. The women promised me the footage wouldn't go anywhere. I believed them. I trusted them – then they wrecked my life and career.'

A few days later, the hotel footage appeared on a sub-scription platform. The man only discovered this when his social-media friends messaged him, saying that they'd seen the video, which had been copied from the website and sent to all his contacts. 'I can't believe this has happened to me,' he said. 'You can only see my face in the video for a fleeting moment, but people recognised me. My colleagues and bosses also saw the footage. I was once a well-respected executive ... now nobody takes me seriously at work.'

It turned out that these two women were targeting men to film sex acts with them – then posting the foot-age on their subscription channels, purely to attract more subscribers and to cash-in on their deeds. 'I feel so embar-rassed, so humiliated,' the executive wrote. 'The footage is still out there. I'm constantly ridiculed over it. Just because I'm a man, it doesn't make it any less painful. I haven't reported this to the police – I'm too ashamed and I don't want more people knowing about the film. I just want this to go away.'

I replied to his message, directing him to the various charities he could speak to, such as SWGfL, who run the Revenge Porn Helpline. The organisation not only offers great support for victims, but can also help with getting explicit footage and images removed from online platforms without charge (I feel extremely lucky that they did this for me). I didn't hear from the man again, but I hope he managed to seek guidance.

Statistics show that one in nine men aged between eighteen and thirty-four have experienced threats to share intimate images. Truthfully, I think this figure is much higher; image-based sexual abuse happens to lots of men, but male victims often don't want to report their cases. They feel too embarrassed to speak about their experiences, but it's important for them to know that they can speak anonymously to charities – and I would strongly advise all victims to do so. I'll say it again: *nobody* should be sharing sexual content of *anyone* without their consent.

Shockingly, revenge porn cases among schoolchildren have rocketed in recent years. I felt sick when I read an article on the Birmingham Live website in June 2023, reporting that a six-year-old had been a victim of this crime. In the report, figures released by West Midlands Police revealed they'd recorded 110 cases of revenge porn between 2021–2022 involving victims aged seventeen and below.

Likewise, a handful of concerned mothers have also

contacted me, saying children as young as twelve have had explicit images of themselves posted online. Other kids have received threats that intimate images of themselves will be leaked – unless they pay a fee to the perpetrator – a crime often labelled 'sextortion'. It disgusts me that the younger generation are becoming victims of revenge porn, but we need to look at why this is happening.

In my early schooldays, we didn't have access to camera phones, social media and apps as children do today. Like I said in my victim-impact statement following Bear's conviction, we are living in an age where so much of our children's lives are spent online – and social media has given us the egalitarian belief that we are all publishers, but what it hasn't done is regulate what we should responsibly publish. Children now have the technology – and ability – to commit these crimes, but I wonder how many who post non-consensual intimate images or footage understand that it's wrong to do so. Teenagers, especially as they become sexually explorative, might not realise they're committing image-based sexual abuse when they upload an explicit picture online – or be aware of the devastating effect that post will have on their victims.

I also think that porn sites, some of which are free and easily accessible, even if you're underaged, are sending out a disturbing message to teenage boys that sex is predominately violent. This is confusing for young men. Some videos on porn sites feature horrific scenes that see men dragging women around the room by their hair or throat as they dominate them during sex. Such footage is warping teenagers' minds when they should be learning how to form loving sexual relationships.

The importance of consent around sharing explicit images needs to be taught to children and young adults. I'm hoping to do talks about this in schools, where I'd tell my story and explain how being a victim of revenge porn has affected me, just as I did in my documentary. I'd enforce the dangers of sending and posting explicit images, and the hurt it can cause, while emphasising how difficult it is to remove this content from online platforms once it's out there. I'd speak about the consequences perpetrators face, using Bear's sentence as an example that you can go to prison for sharing non-consensual sexual-based images. I'm determined to make my story resonate with the younger generations.

Some social-media platforms completely facilitate porn. I regularly see this on Twitter and TikTok – people using their accounts to direct followers to their subscription porn channels. Bear did this during his trial: on Twitter, he uploaded a picture of himself stepping out of his hired Rolls Royce outside Chelmsford Crown Court with the accompanying text: *50% off my adult site for the next 24 hours. Come see why I'm trending.* That wasn't the first time Bear had promoted his home videos on social media. Prior to his trial, in August 2021, he shared an X-rated clip on Twitter titled 'Showers hit different abroad', showing his girlfriend performing a sex act on him in a bathroom. That trending footage, which Bear's girlfriend shared with a link to her porn site, was viewed by millions. Her porn site was removed but the video remained on social media, prompting a public petition to 'stop Stephen Bear from posting pornographic content on Twitter'. Naturally, people were outraged that this content was in the public domain. The age limit for Twitter is thirteen, and once a post goes viral – as Bear's did – it invariably appears on users' timelines, meaning young people can stumble upon it all too easily.

Admittedly, Bear's videos with his girlfriend were consensual, but the use of social media and video-sharing channels for image-based sexual abuse is massive. In relationships, it's terrifyingly easy for a partner to post sexual content online – and nowadays everyone has access to these platforms at the drop of a hat.

This was even more prevalent during the pandemic. Lockdown triggered a surge in revenge porn cases as people furthered and formed relationships online. Data released by the Metropolitan Police revealed a 329 per cent rise in offences in London between 1 October 2020 and 31 October 2021. The Revenge Porn Helpline saw cases of image-based sexual abuse double, and sextortion incidents triple in that year. The helpline also said that an average of forty-two images were recorded following reports from women, compared to less than two for male victims.

Even after Covid restrictions were lifted, cases of revenge porn remained high. The rise in adult-only subscription channels has fuelled this trend by giving perpetrators a monetary incentive. Some abusers are targeting their victims, too, with the aim of growing their own audiences.

These platforms need to be held accountable when

non-consensual content is reported to them. I'm thrilled to hear that the government is tabling another amendment to the Online Safety Bill, which will see companies facing fines of up to 10 per cent of their global turnover if they fail to ban repeat offenders or to remove abusive misogynistic content. However, I firmly believe that subscription platforms have the finance, ability and algorithms to help prevent this material from appearing on their sites in the first place. Maybe these channels could install a technology that flags up videos and images featuring more than one person. Then the verified account holder could be contacted and asked whether the other individuals have consented to the posted content. Or perhaps a system could be implemented wherein all participants must give their written consent, along with proof of identification, before an image or video is posted? And when revenge porn cases are flagged, I believe the website should pause this content and conduct a full investigation into the matter.

It's life-changing when somebody sends graphic footage or pictures of you into cyberspace for the whole world to see. It's propagated at lightning speed, can be shared by millions of internet users, and even if some sites do remove the offending picture or video, it will invariably pop up on yet another platform. It's virtually impossible to completely eradicate such matter – I know that Bear's garden footage still lurks in corners of the web.

In a previous chapter I spoke about Victoria, whose ex-partner, Stuart Gaunt, secretly filmed her naked in the shower before uploading screenshots of the clip on to a porn website. He got a suspended jail sentence for voyeurism but wasn't charged with putting the images online or ordered to take them down. In the eyes of the law, Gaunt filmed the footage and therefore owns copyright.

Victoria took her case to the High Court in February 2023, and won almost £100,000 in damages for her psychiatric injury and to pay for a specialist company to remove the images. However, when I spoke to Victoria in May 2023, she said the images were still on some sites. She told me how she felt physically and mentally violated after Gaunt, a man she'd once loved and trusted, released the screenshots. 'I needed to know that all these pictures could be removed,' she said. 'The thought of sitting next to someone on the train who had seen the footage made me feel physically sick.

'It feels wrong that even with a criminal conviction there is no requirement to remove offensive content. That cannot be right. In time, I would like to see the onus taken off victims to pursue redress.'

I agree wholeheartedly with Victoria. It seems wrong that, despite gaining a conviction for voyeurism, Gaunt's pictures were still deemed legal. I think the government should act on this to ensure that platforms immediately remove non-consensual images, especially in cases where the perpetrator is convicted.

As Alex Chalk pointed out during our meeting in June 2023, technology is always going to be one step ahead of the law. This means that keeping up with rapid technological advances is challenging for the government.

Looking ahead, I'd like to think that, in ten years' time, there will be more restrictions in place regarding the kinds of content social-media and subscription companies allow on their sites. I hope that the heads of these platforms will have open discussions with victims, politicians, and charities, and show they are willing – from the bottom of their hearts – to ensure whatever happens on their pages is safe for their users. Additionally, I expect companies to respond rapidly to reports of revenge porn in the future. There should be a human being, not a robot, available to deal with these enquiries – within twenty-four hours.

Communication is key to preventing image-based sexual abuse. People need to speak out, to voice their fears and report these crimes, and the government needs to listen. But thankfully, the government *is* listening to the public; it *is* taking this matter seriously.

As the Online Safety Bill passes through the House of Lords, the government has made further amendments to 'protect children and empower adults'. The bill will introduce age verification for sites hosting porn, which the government says will probably involve facial-recognition identification. Senior managers at technology platforms, including social-media companies, could face up to two years in jail if they ignore warnings about child-safety breaches from the communications watchdog, Ofcom. These are huge steps in the right direction towards making the internet a safe space where young people can interact.

*

My revenge porn trauma will never fully leave me. As I've said before, Bear took away my innocent spark from the moment he put that video online. Recovering from image-based sexual abuse is a grieving process; it's like losing a close friend or family member. The emotions really do hit you in waves, and my advice to other victims is to acknowledge these emotions, to understand that they're natural feelings that will pass with time – because all things do pass with time. You've just got to be patient with yourself.

I'm pleased to say, though, that the Bear episode has made me stronger and more resilient. I've regained my confidence and I feel really happy with my life.

Campaigning for the amendment to the Online Safety Bill – and securing a change in the law – meant the world to me, and I'll continue to help and listen to other victims.

To anyone else who's going through this horrendous ordeal, I reiterate: you have nothing to be ashamed of; the only person who should feel shame is the person who posted the pictures or footage online. And please, don't suffer in silence. It's really important that you reach out for help. Even if you don't wish to go to the police, there are plenty of charities you can speak to anonymously.

But for victims who do want to seek criminal justice, I urge you to do so. You no longer have to prove that your abuser caused you harm or distress. It's there in black and white – we've rewritten the law. Remember: it's *your* body, *your* consent. Now, go for it. Take back *your* power.

ACKNOWLEDGEMENTS

Where do I start? There are so many people I want to thank, so, here goes:

A huge thanks to Essex Police, especially to DC Brian Sitch for ensuring the truth was revealed.

From the bottom of my heart, thank you to my amazing family – Mum; Dad; my stepmum, Leigh; my sisters, Darcey and Eva Harrison; and my brother, Danny Harrison; Nanny Colleen; Nanny Flo; Aunty Sharon; and Uncle Danny. Thank you to my cousins, Sian, Conner, Bryn; Aunty Julie; and Uncle Paul. Special thanks also to Michelle Roycroft and Michelle Sugar for being by my side in court and supporting Mum.

To Matthew Redden, thank you for your assistance in removing the footage from various websites and your help during the court case.

I want to thank all my amazing friends for pulling me through and making me laugh, even when the tears streamed down my face. To Bella Kempley, Tyla and Star Jones, Rachel Luton, Nicole Charbass, Jamie Charbass, Fran Parman, Clelia Theodorou, Olivia Attwood, Lara

Accinson, Kaz Crossley, James Argent, Ahmad Harb, Ayman Harb, Juliet Sosa, Sarah Devermont, Montana Brown, Brooke Chamberlain, Kamoon, Alex Swallow, Jordan Dale and Theo Campbell – you're all the best friends in the world.

Massive thanks to my girls' mums, too, Lisa Kempley and Joanne Wooder – for helping me through my grief.

Thank you to my agent, Neil Dobias at Force 1 Management, for supporting me as a friend when I needed you, and also in business.

To the team at Payne Hicks Beach for my legal support – and to Caroline Nokes, Ed Balls, Yvette Cooper, Jess Phillips, Keir Starmer, Alex Chalk and Edward Argar for assisting me in the political sector. I would also like to thank Laura Kuenssberg for inviting me on to her show – this really kick-started my campaign.

I'd like to thank my literary agent, Oscar Janson-Smith, for making this book possible. Huge thanks also to Christina Demosthenous and the talented team at Renegade Books for their vision to bring this book to life. Thank you, Nicola Stow, for being such an amazing writer and dedicating your time to making this book so special.

I want to thank Cenk and Jake's amazing families for raising two men who helped contribute so much to the person I have become today. May you all continue to heal from your loss.

To the team at MultiStory Media and ITV who helped bring my documentary to life – especially Kate Teckman, Ceri Aston, Fabian Bohan-Taghian and Candace Davies.

And, finally, thank you to Jason Vale and the entire team at No1 Boot Camp – visiting Juicy Oasis and No1 multiple times has really helped me to navigate my journey and get back on track.

Bringing a book from manuscript to what you are reading is a team effort.

Renegade Books would like to thank everyone who helped to publish *Taking Back My Power*.

Editorial
Christina Demosthenous

Production
Narges Nojoumi

Contracts
Megan Phillips
Amy Patrick
Anne Goddard
Bryony Hall
Sasha Duszynska Lewis

Publicity
Millie Seaward

Marketing
Emily Moran

Sales
Caitriona Row
Dominic Smith
Frances Doyle
Hannah Methuen
Lucy Hine
Toluwalope Ayo-Ajala

Operations
Kellie Barnfield
Millie Gibson
Sameera Patel
Sanjeev Braich

Finance
Andrew Smith
Ellie Barry

Design
Charlotte Stroomer